Basic Idioms In American English

BOOK 2

HUBERT H. SETZLER, JR.

SCIENCE RESEARCH ASSOCIATES, INC.
Chicago, Palo Alto, Toronto, Henley-on-Thames, Sydney

A Subsidiary of IBM

Illustrations by Sedonia Champlain
Cover design by Caroff/Reiken

Published by
Science Research Associates, Inc.
155 North Wacker Drive
Chicago, Illinois 60606

ISBN: 0-574-16013-2

Printed in the United States of America

Preface

This is the second of a two-book series entitled *Basic Idioms in American English*. They are intended for students of English as a foreign language. Idioms are a constant source of difficulty for non-native speakers of English since direct translations often prove nonsensical and misleading. However, mastery of the most commonly used idiomatic expressions is essential for natural, everyday communication. The idioms contained in these two books have been selected for their high frequency and are constantly used by most Americans in their daily lives. Each lesson includes dialogues based on actual conversations, interviews, recorded by the author. These interviews accurately reflect the living language of Americans of all ages and walks of life.

The books are divided into modules of four lessons each. Each lesson begins with a dialogue which introduces the new idioms in context. This is followed by an alphabetically-arranged list of all new idioms with their respective definitions and two or more sample sentences. Then the student is asked to use the idioms in a variety of exercises.

Each module is a self-contained learning unit, that is, the student does not need to learn the first module in order to study the second one. The modules are independent, as are the lessons, but they are presented in a suggested sequence. Teachers and learners of English can easily adapt the lessons to their own curriculum, interests, or individual needs.

Books 1 and 2 are similar in all respects. The eight modules of Book 1 are COME TO YOUR SENSES, PERSON TO PERSON, TIME AND TIME AGAIN, START TO FINISH, ODDS AND ENDS, DAILY ACTIVITIES, IN THE EVENING, and OCCASIONS.

Only extensive drill and practice will bring complete mastery of the many idiomatic expressions of the English language. Our goal in these books has been to make this task enjoyable and rewarding.

Contents

Lesson 1: Types and Traits: What People Are

Interview

This interview took place beside the swimming pool with three women—Joan, Margaret, and Jackie. The swimming pool is the heart of the Community Club. During the summer most of the mothers and fathers bring their children to the club for a swim.

Joan: Oh, no! Here he comes with that tape recorder again. Well, what are you up to this time?

Int: Nothing much. I just want to ask you a few questions about the kinds of people you have at the club. You know, about their personalities.

Mar: Of course, all of our members are wonderful! And we have all kinds of different personalities. We have a very **open-minded** policy.

Jackie: Ha, Margaret! We have the most **narrow-minded** people in town. I have never seen such a bunch of **stuffed shirts** and **windbags.**

1

Mar: That's not true, Jackie. You're just being **hard-hearted.** We do have many fine members. Take Sharon over there—a real **live wire.** She's so witty and clever. She makes me feel like a **wet blanket.**

Joan: Yes, she is. And her husband is a **self-made** man. He started with almost nothing and worked his way to the top. Now he's **a man of means.**

Jackie: You're too **soft-hearted.** Sharon's husband thinks he's a **big shot,** but he's just a **yes-man.** I don't know where you get those **hare-brained** ideas. You're usually so **level-headed.**

Mar: Jackie! Don't be so **pig-headed!**

A man/woman of means *a wealthy person*

Once I was poor, but now I'm **a man of means!** My aunt died and left me a fortune.

Big shot *an important person*

Juan is a **big shot** in local politics.

Hard-hearted *without pity, merciless*

A **hard-hearted** person rarely gives money to charity.

Hare-brained *foolish, thoughtless*

Many of the world's great geniuses were thought to be **hare-brained** when they were children.

Level-headed *self-composed and sensible*

Gloria is always calm in every situation. She is the most **level-headed** person I know.

Live wire *an energetic, active person*

Howard is a **live wire** business executive. He works from morning to night.

2

Narrow-minded   *bigoted, having a limited outlook*

George is not a bad person. He's just **narrow-minded.**

Open-minded   *liberal, having a liberal, open outlook*

A truly **open-minded** person respects the beliefs of others.

Pig-headed   *stubborn*

My father won't let me use his car tonight. I wish he weren't so **pig-headed.**

Self-made   *having achieved success without the help of others*

Self-made men and women succeed without the help of others.

Soft-hearted   *tender, merciful, generous*

Students often take advantage of **soft-hearted** teachers.

Stuffed shirt   *a pompous, boring person*

The mayor thinks he's an important man, but he's really a **stuffed shirt.**

Wet blanket   *a person who discourages enthusiasm or enjoyment*

Ann sulked during the entire movie. None of us could enjoy the show. She was such a **wet blanket.**

Windbag   *a talkative, boring person*

That's the longest, most boring speech I ever heard. I thought the old **windbag** would never shut up.

Yes-man   *a person who always agrees with his boss or superior*

Give me a strong, independent leader. I don't want a bunch of **yes-men.**

Exercise

Check the idioms that *might* describe the person or persons in the pictures. Check as many idioms as you like for each picture. Explain why you selected each idiom.

- ☐ pig-headed
- ☐ soft-hearted
- ☒ hare-brained
- ☐ live wire
- ☐ narrow-minded

- ☐ open-minded
- ☐ wet blanket
- ☐ hard-hearted
- ☐ pig-headed
- ☒ narrow-minded

- ☐ level-headed
- ☐ windbag
- ☐ open-minded
- ☐ big shot
- ☒ woman of means

- ☒ yes-man
- ☒ stuffed shirt
- ☐ level-headed
- ☐ wet blanket
- ☐ live wire

- ☐ yes-man
- ☐ self-made
- ☐ wet blanket
- ☒ windbag
- ☐ stuffed shirt

PRESIDENT

- ☐ big shot
- ☐ soft-hearted
- ☐ hard-hearted
- ☐ man of means
- ☒ self-made

4

Lesson 2: Types and Traits: What People Do

This interview is a continuation of the earlier conversation. Joan, Margaret, and Jackie explain the meanings of some of the idioms used earlier.

Inter: A little while ago you were describing people as live wires, wet blankets, soft-hearted, and so on. What exactly do these words mean to you?

Mar: Well, let's see. A live wire is a person with a lot of energy like Jackie. She's always **on the go.**

Jackie: Yes, and Margaret is soft-hearted. She can **be taken in** by anyone. She's a real **pushover.**

Joan: I call you pig-headed, Jackie. That means you were stubborn. You **were dead set against** anything we said.

Mar: A yes-man or woman is someone who does whatever he or she is told. Yes-men and women are **under the thumb** of their bosses all of the time.

Joan: That's what Jackie said about Sharon's husband. Well, he **is** a man of means and he is **well off!**

Mar: **Don't waste your breath,** Joan. Jackie **looks down on** practically everyone.

Jackie: Why, you've **got me all wrong** ! I **think highly** of most people. However, I must **point out** that Sharon is quite a **social climber,** now that her husband **is well off.**

Joan: Oh, Jackie! You're impossible! Everything you say has **to be taken with a grain of salt!**

Be dead set against   *to be much opposed to*

Many young people **are dead set against** the military draft.

Be taken in   *to be deceived*

Many children and adults **are taken in** by the clever ads on television.

Be well off   *to be rich, to have more than is necessary*

Carlos is no millionaire, but he certainly **is well off.**

Get (someone/something) wrong   *to misunderstand*

I prefer to read, rather than watch television. **Don't get me wrong!** I like television, but I like reading better.

Look down on (someone)   *to consider someone inferior*

Snobs are people who **look down on** others.

On the go   *very active*

Maria is busy all the time. I wonder where she gets the energy to stay **on the go** the way she does.

Point out   *to indicate, to bring attention to*

Please **point out** my mistakes in this writing assignment. **Point** them **out** in red pencil.

Pushover *someone who is easy to influence or manipulate*

Robert believes anything you say. He really is a **pushover.**

Social climber *someone who actively seeks to elevate his or her social position*

In any society there are those **social climbers** who wish to be highly thought of by the company they keep.

Take (someone/something) with a grain of salt *to accept with reservations, to believe only in part*

George likes to make up those stories he tells. You must **take** what he says **with a grain of salt.**

Think highly of *to hold in esteem*

The students **think highly of** their English teacher.

Under (one's) thumb *under one's domination*

I don't know why, but I do everything she tells me to do. I'm afraid she has me **under her thumb.**

Waste (one's) breath *to lose one's time and effort arguing*

Don't **waste your breath,** she'll never listen to anyone.

Exercise 1

In each of the following scenes, select the idiom that best completes each blank.

a. Heather is fifteen years old. She wants to travel to New York by herself. "No," said her mother, "_____ ."
(1) I think highly of New York (2) I'm dead set against it
(3) Take me with a grain of salt

b. Larry always criticized Chuck. Larry thought Chuck couldn't do anything right. Finally, Chuck said, "Let me _____ that everyone makes mistakes!"

(1) point out (2) look down on (3) be taken in

c. The older teacher told the new teacher that all the students were fine boys and girls. "You may not think so, but all your students are smart," remarked the older teacher. The new teacher said, "Actually, _____ ."

(1) I'm a social climber   (2) these students are always on the go   (3) I think highly of all my students

d. A door-to-door salesman sold Harvey a twenty-piece set of cookware. Later Harvey realized that he didn't even like to cook. Harvey said to himself, "How could I _____ ?"

(1) point out that salesman   (2) waste my breath with that salesman   (3) be taken in by that salesman

e. Antonio tried to convince Walter to stop smoking. Helen told Antonio not to argue with Walter. Helen said, "Don't waste your breath with Walter. _____ ."

(1) He's a pushover   (2) He's on the go   (3) He's too pig-headed

f. Aunt Lou was worried about her bills—telephone bills, food bills, clothing bills, and taxes. Her daughter said, "Mother, how can you complain? You're a wealthy woman." Aunt Lou replied, "Well, I'm not rich, but I suppose _____ ."

(1) I'm well off   (2) I'm a pushover   (3) I'm under his thumb

2. **Match the following idioms from column 1 and column 2 to make a complete sentence.**

Column 1	Column 2
____ A social climber	a. is well off.
____ A pushover	b. is always on the go.
____ A live wire	c. sometimes looks down on others.
____ A yes-man	d. must be taken with a grain of salt.
____ A hare-brained person	e. is under his superior's thumb.
____ A man of means	f. is easily taken in.

8

Lesson 3: Likable and Trustworthy People

Interview

This is the last part of the interview with Joan, Margaret, and Jackie. They are discussing the admirable qualities of the club director.

Mar: I think Jackie has been too hard on the people we know here. Most of them have a lot **on the ball.** We **have what it takes** to make this a fine Community Club, a recreation center for everyone.

Joan: Margaret's right. We have a lot of new members. Our director, Scott McKay, **has a good head on his shoulders** and he **was** certainly **cut out for** the job of director.

Jackie: Well, you're right about him. Whenever Scott plans something, he **goes whole hog.** Everyone **raved about** the way the tennis tournament was run. Scott **went out of his way** to see that everyone had a good time.

Mar: Yes, he did. You know he had trouble when he first came here. Most of the members didn't think he could

9

stand on his own two feet. Some people complained a lot. Scott is very level-headed and **took it on the chin** without a word. He proved he could do a good job.

Jackie: I have to admit Scott was a **late bloomer.** But he made this an **up-to-date** club. He made it a club you can **take pride in.**

Cut out for   *to be suited for*

Just because Robert likes music and poetry, you think he **isn't cut out for** sports.

Go out of (one's) way   *to make a special effort*

Lois **went out of her way** to invite George to the party and he still didn't come.

Go whole hog   *to do something thoroughly*

When Rachel and Bob throw a party, they **go whole hog.**

Have a good head on (one's) shoulders   *to be intelligent and practical*

The first requirement for this job is that you **have a good head on your shoulders.**

Have what it takes   *to have the required intelligence, ability, or courage*

To be successful in major league baseball, you must **have what it takes.**

Late bloomer   *someone who does not achieve at first, but later becomes very proficient or successful*

Antonio had trouble with his English at first, but now he is the best student in class. He was definitely a **late bloomer.**

On the ball   *alert, attentive*

If you are going to run for office and talk to a number of newspaper reporters, you must always stay **on the ball.**

Rave about   *to talk enthusiastically about*

The boss **raved about** the growth in sales this month.

Stand on (one's) own two feet   *to be independent*

Children are dependent on their parents. Adults must learn **to stand on their own two feet.**

Take it on the chin   *to suffer abuse without complaint*

The angry motorist screamed at the police officer, but the officer **took it on the chin.**

Take pride in   *to be proud of, to gain satisfaction from*

Everyone should **take pride in** his or her country.

Up-to-date   *modern*

This is a very **up-to-date** school. Did you see all the new equipment, the big library, and the number of new teachers?

Exercise

Study each picture. Select one idiom for each picture and make a statement that helps describe the picture.

cut out for, have what it takes, take it on the chin

late bloomer, stand on one's own two feet, have a good head on one's shoulders

rave about, take pride in, on the ball

go whole hog, up-to-date

Lesson 4: As Good As Your Word

Interview

The interviewer now speaks with the husbands of Joan, Margaret, and Jackie—Bob, Pete, and Howard. They have just returned from their tennis match.

Interviewer: Excuse me, gentlemen. May I **have a word with** you? I've been talking with your wives about the kinds of people we have around here. Now I'd like to get your opinions.

Howard: Sure thing. When Jackie's around I hardly **get a word in edgewise.** I only get to say things **under my breath.**

Bob: What do you want to know? I'd like to **have a say** in this, too.

Interviewer: Your wives were expressing their opinions about our director, Scott.

Pete: I don't know what they said, but **take my word** for it, Scott's a great guy. I didn't think so at first, but I surely have had to **eat my words.**

13

Interviewer: In other words, you fellows are pleased with the job Scott is doing.

Howard: Absolutely. Yes, absolutely. Scott **gave us his word** that he would make this a first-rate club. We found out that he doesn't **break his word.**

Bob: That's right. And he has some new plans coming up. Some of his ideas can **take your breath away. Mark my words,** if we don't vote him a raise in salary, we'll soon lose him to another club.

Pete: Yes, I agree.

As good as (one's) word *reliable, dependable, trustworthy*

You can trust Barbara to be here on time. She's **as good as her word.**

Break (one's) word *to fail to fulfill a promise*

After all the promises the candidate made, she never **broke her word** to a single voter.

Eat (one's) words *to apologize humbly, to retract*

Don't criticize people too often; you may have **to eat your words.**

Get a word in edgewise *to enter a conversation with difficulty*

Allen talked all evening without stopping. I couldn't **get a word in edgewise!**

Give (one's) word *to promise*

Cherie didn't want to go to the movies this evening, but she **had** already **given her word** to the children.

Have a say in *to have some input into, to have some influence in*

If you are going to hire someone, we want **to have a say in** who gets the job.

Have a word with *to talk or discuss briefly*

Before we go into the meeting, may I **have a word with** you?

In other words   *a different way of saying it*

You said that the salary is unsatisfactory. **In other words**, you want more money.

Mark (one's) words   *to pay close attention to what one says*

Mark my words, you'll be speaking English fluently within a year.

Take (one's) breath away   *to astonish, to overwhelm*

The sunset was so beautiful. The view **took my breath away**.

Take (one's) word (for)   *to accept or believe one's promise*

Take my word for it, computers and electronics are the basis of all future progress.

Under (one's) breath   *in a whisper*

Although Helen was angry with her supervisor, she didn't say anything to him. She just walked away mumbling **under her breath**.

Exercise

Select the correct idiom to complete each sentence.

a. _____ , Larry paid his debts when they came due.

  (1) Eating his words   (2) As good as his word

  (3) Under his breath

b. I could not hear what Carmen said. She said something ____
  _____ .

  (1) in other words   (2) as good as her word   (3) under her breath

c. Alice refused to go to Europe. _____ , Alice doesn't like to travel.

  (1) In other words   (2) As good as her word   (3) Under her breath

15

d. Barbara's boss is an old windbag. She doesn't like to talk to him. Barbara can't _____ .

   (1) get a word in edgewise   (2) eat her words   (3) break her word

e. You shouldn't criticize her work. You may have to _____ _____ .

   (1) get a word in edgewise   (2) eat your words
   (3) break your word

f. Don't promise what you can't deliver. You should never _____ _____ .

   (1) get a word in edgewise   (2) eat your words
   (3) break your word

g. _____ , by the end of the school year George will have the best grades.

   (1) Take my breath away   (2) Mark my words
   (3) Give my word

h. Your car will be repaired by tomorrow. I_____.

   (1) take your breath away   (2) mark your words
   (3) give you my word

i. The music was so beautiful, it _____ .

   (1) took my breath away   (2) mark my words
   (3) give you my word

j. In a democracy everyone wants to _____ the government.

   (1) take your word for   (2) have a word with
   (3) have a say in

k. I trust you completely. If you say so, I'll _____it.

   (1) take your word for   (2) have a word with
   (3) have a say in

l. Excuse me, Helen. May I _____ you?

   (1) take your word for   (2) have a word with
   (3) have a say in

Lesson 1: Remembering and Forgetting

Interview

The interviewer went to a supermarket, the *Big W*, to find out how people remember and forget things. Supermarkets have a wide variety of foods, cooking utensils, household goods, medical supplies, health and grooming aids, and many other items. American shoppers find that supermarkets are the most economical way to shop. Because there are so many things in today's supermarkets, most people make out a shopping list to help them remember what they need to buy.

The interviewer has just stopped a couple to ask them about how they shop. Bill and Ann do their shopping on Friday evenings. They buy most of their groceries for the coming week.

Ann: So that is a survey about remembering and forgetting things. I thought you were one of those television advertising men. You're sure we aren't going to be on T.V.?

17

Interviewer: No, I'm afraid not. This is a simple survey on how you shop. How do you remember what to buy with so many things available in the store?

Ann: You know, it's really hard. There's so much stuff to choose from. I'm so **absent-minded,** I make out a shopping list like this one. This way I can **keep track of** what I need and what I intend to buy.

Bill: Yes, Ann is a very efficient shopper. I, on the other hand, buy whatever **crosses my mind.**

Ann: That's true. Bill thinks he knows **by heart** what we need and what we don't. He sees something on the shelf and it **rings a bell.** Then he runs off to buy whatever he has forgotten.

Bill: Well, I'm like most people. You see something and it reminds you of something else you've forgotten.

Ann: Yes, but sometimes you buy things we really don't need. With so many choices, you can easily **get mixed up.** You have to **bear in mind** that we have **just so much** money to spend on food. You can't just buy anything that **pops into your head!**

Interviewer: Are you saying that you can **lose sight of** why you came into the store?

Bill: Oh, yes. That happens to me a lot. I can't seem to **keep in mind** why I came in.

Ann: That's the truth! Last week Bill went to the store to get three jars of baby food. He came home with potato chips, onion dip, and a six-pack of soda. Of course, the baby food never **came to mind!**

Interviewer: You forgot the baby food? How could that happen, Bill?

Bill: **Search me.** I guess the sight of the potato chips **brought to mind** the fun Ann and I have just relaxing together in front of the T.V.

18

Absent-minded   *forgetful*

In America there are many jokes about **absent-minded** professors.

Bear in mind   *to remember*

Bear in mind that you promised to babysit for me this evening.

Bring to mind   *to remind*

My son's graduation **brought to mind** my own school days.

By heart   *from memory*

Baseball fans can learn every score for the whole season **by heart.**

Come to mind   *to be recalled, remembered*

I knew that I met him once before, but his name wouldn't **come to mind.**

Cross (one's) mind   *to occur in one's mind, to be thought of*

I knew that restaurant was popular, but it didn't **cross my mind** to make reservations.

Get mixed up   *to become confused*

Every time my boss explains the new sales plan, I **get mixed up.**

Just so much   *a specific or limited amount*

We couldn't buy it. We had **just so much** to spend.

Keep in mind   *to remember constantly*

When you go swimming here, you should **keep in mind** that the water is swift.

Keep track of   *to monitor*

Baseball fans often **keep track of** every team in the league.

Lose sight of   *to fail to remember, to fail to keep track of*

Carmen does many different things, but she never **loses sight** of her ultimate goal.

Pop into (one's) head   *to become an immediate thought or idea in someone's mind*

Henry is very unpredictable. He says anything that **pops into his head.**

Ring a bell   *to remind someone of something*

I'm not sure I know who you are talking about, but the name **rings a bell.**

Search me!   *I don't know (used informally)*

Search me! I don't know the answer.

Exercise 1

Choose the correct definition for the following idioms.

a. lose sight of

   (1) to remind someone of something   (2) to fail to remember
   (3) by memory   (4) to occur in one's mind

b. absent-minded

   (1) not knowing   (2) having a thought or idea
   (3) forgetful   (4) mindful

c. by heart

   (1) bravely   (2) from memory
   (3) by repetition   (4) emotionally

d. get mixed up

   (1) forget   (2) recall   (3) become confused
   (4) be in trouble

e. ring a bell

   (1) from memory   (2) fail to remember
   (3) remind someone of something   (4) monitor

f. keep in mind

   (1) remember constantly   (2) become confused
   (3) by memory   (4) occur in one's mind

Exercise 2

Substitute the proper idiom for the word or words or phrase in parentheses.

a. **(I don't know!)** I don't understand the question.

b. Spring always **(reminds me of)** songs of love.

c. I can remember his name, but his address **(isn't recalled).**

d. When you ask her a question she usually says the first thing that **(becomes immediately thought of).**

e. It's hard **(to monitor)** all these children all day long.

f. When you judge his work you must **(remember)** his inexperience.

g. It **(occurred in my mind)** to call Sarah, but I got busy and soon forgot.

Lesson 2: Belief and Opinion

Interviews

The interviewer stopped several people in front of the supermarket. He asked them about their opinions of the advantages and disadvantages of shopping at a supermarket.

A businessman in his fifties.

Interviewer: And you, sir. What do you think of shopping in supermarkets.

Man: Well, let me see. I'd have to **think twice about** that. Supermarkets are convenient because you can buy **just about** anything you want. I wish they wouldn't **dream up** so many different brand names for the same thing. For example, I could shop for a year and never buy the same brand of corn flakes. Now that isn't necessary. **As far as** I'm concerned, corn flakes are corn flakes.

A homemaker with three children.

Homemaker: Oh, supermarkets are **right up my alley.** I have three children to shop for. **By no stretch of the imagination** could I survive without the convenience of the supermarket. It also saves me time and money.

A woman with a six-pack of club soda.

Woman: Supermarkets are okay. I like them. Today is different, though. Today I don't like this supermarket **in view of** the fact that all I wanted was this six-pack. But I had to wait in line at the check-out counter for ten minutes. I feel that was a waste of time. I **draw the line** at that kind of waiting around. Of course, tomorrow I do my weekly shopping. Supermarkets are great for that! I suppose I'll **change my tune** tomorrow.

A farmer in his early thirties.

Farmer: I **take a dim view of** all that advertising. With all of the different claims those ads make I can't seem **to make up my mind.** I want **to make certain** I'm getting the best buy for my money. Those ads **are** always **changing my mind.** Sometimes I really get confused.

As far as I'm concerned *in my opinion*

As far as I'm concerned, Mary Alice is a good teacher.

By no stretch of the imagination *by no possible attempt or effort*

By no stretch of the imagination can Jim become an astronaut. He doesn't even like to fly.

Change (one's) mind *to alter one's opinion or plan*

No, Franco isn't going with us. He said he was going, but he **changed his mind.**

Change (one's) tune *to alter one's attitude*

Barbara hated to travel. But after her trip to Japan, she **changed her tune.**

Draw the line at *to reach one's limit*

I eat junk foods regularly, but I **draw the line at** smoking.

Dream up *to invent, to think up*

My teenage son can **dream up** a hundred ways to ask for money.

In view of *considering, in consideration of*

In view of the gas shortage, I'm going to buy a compact car this year.

Just about *almost*

We arrived **just about** on time.

Make certain *to be sure, to be positive*

Helen **made certain** that everyone was clear about the job requirements.

Make up (one's) mind *to decide*

I hate to go shopping with Eddy. He can never **make up his mind** whether he wants to buy something or not.

Right up (one's) alley *in one's area of interest or skill*

Of course Reggie is a good tennis player. All sports are **right up his alley**.

Take a dim view of *to have a low opinion of, to be skeptical about*

The American public now **takes a dim view of** owning a large car. More and more people are buying small cars.

Think twice about *to consider carefully*

If you do buy a large car, you had better **think twice about** going on long trips.

Exercise

Study each picture. Select one idiom for each picture and make a statement that helps describe the picture.

24

As far as I'm concerned, by no stretch of the imagination

Dream up, just about, right up one's alley

Make certain, think twice about, make up one's mind

take a dim view of, change one's mind

Lesson 3: Understanding

Interview

The interviewer talks with the manager of the local *Big W*. His name is Donald Cromer. The conversation is about the problem of how a large supermarket meets all the needs of its customers.

Interviewer: One of the main complaints I heard was there were too many choices. I know it **doesn't make sense,** but that is what a lot of people told me.

Don: Yes, that's right. **It stands to reason** that too many choices are as bad as too few.

Interviewer: Yes, there are so many brand names that a simple task like shopping for groceries becomes complicated.

Don: You have obviously **sized up** the problem and I think you **get the picture.** You **catch on** pretty fast.

Interviewer: What do you do to keep all the customers satisfied?

Don: Well, the big shots in management **have kicked this problem around** for years. Finally, they **came to their senses. If you know the first thing about** the supermarket business, you know that customers want variety, economy, and convenience. **Put that together** and what do you get?

Interviewer: **As a rule,** I'd say that means a large inventory, low prices, and quick service.

Don: **Without question,** that's what it means. But that **raises the question** of how to give the customers what they want.

Interviewer: What are you doing about that?

Don: We've **taken steps** to improve all of our services. We have larger stores. We use computerized check-out service. We have an express check-out line for customers with fewer than ten items. We even use computers to keep track of inventory.

Interviewer: That's why shopping is faster and more convenient now.

Don: Right! We **beat our brains out** for years trying to solve the problem. Now computers are helping us **put two and two together.** We get better and better every year!

As a rule   *generally*

As a rule, most people take their vacations in the summer.

Beat one's brains out   *to think desperately and work feverishly*

I **beat my brains out** trying to find the solution to that algebra problem.

Catch on   *to understand, to grasp the point of*

Algebra is a hard subject. At first I **didn't catch on** at all. Later I began to understand the logic of it.

Come to (one's) senses   *to become reasonable, logical, or sensible*

Joan used to spend her money on silly things of no value. Now she's quite thrifty. I'm glad Joan finally **came to her senses.**

Get the picture   *to understand*

If you don't study idioms, you can't expect to learn to speak English. **Do you get the picture?**

It stands to reason   *to be clear and logical*

It stands to reason that drinking and smoking can ruin your health.

Kick something around   *to discuss an idea or concept*

Before we decide where we are going on our vacation, let's **kick it around** for a while.

Know the first thing about   *to really understand, to know the most important things about*

How can Sarah and David get married so young? They **don't know the first thing about** marriage!

Make sense   *to be intelligible or understandable*

She is an experienced business woman. When she speaks, she **makes sense.**

Put together   *to assemble*

Elena helped her son **put together** his new model airplane.

Put two and two together   *to deduce, to draw a conclusion from observations*

I couldn't understand the directions for putting together the model. First I studied the directions and then I inspected the parts of the plane. Finally, I was able **to put two and two together.**

Raise the question   *to present something for discussion, to ask about*

After the committee planned to build new tennis courts for the community, Aki **raised the question** of money.

Size someone/something up   *to evaluate, estimate, comprehend*

I **sized up** the audience as I spoke on the dangers of alcoholism. I could feel them **sizing me up** too.

Take steps   *to do what is necessary*

My boss **took steps** to see that I got a raise.

Without question   *undoubtedly*

Without quesfion, Larry is the best student in class.

Exercise 1

Replace the boldface words and phrases with the correct idiom.

Roger went into the office to see his math teacher. He was upset. "**Undoubtedly** these are the hardest algebra problems I ever saw. I just **don't have any understanding of** algebra." The teacher smiled and said, "All right, Roger. Let's **discuss these problems** for a few minutes. Let's see if we can **draw any conclusions from what we know.**"

It turned out that Roger **had worked desperately** on converting fractions to decimals. He thought he **had grasped the point on** how to convert fractions, but he had not. Unfortunately, he **had not understood.** His teacher explained it to him again. Now Roger is pleased with his work.

had beat his brains out	had caught on
put two and two together	don't know the first thing about
hadn't gotten the picture	kick these problems around
without question	

Exercise 2

Read the sentences and select the correct idiom to replace the boldface word or phrase.

a. **Generally,** I don't like to eat spicy foods.

   (1) Without question   (2) As a rule   (3) It stands to reason

b. What an argument! Yet Eric **was reasonable in the end.**

   (1) stood to reason   (2) raised the question
   (3) came to his senses

29

c. Janine is great to work with. When she speaks, she is **intelligible.**

(1) makes sense   (2) stands to reason   (3) takes steps

d. If you buy the parts for the sailboat, **I'll assemble them.**

(1) I'll take the steps   (2) I'll put them together
(3) I'll make sense out of them

e. I thought everyone understood the rules until Bill **asked about** time limits.

(1) raised the question of   (2) made sense of
(3) caught on

f. Don't do anything until we **evaluate** the situation.

(1) catch on   (2) make sense of   (3) size up

g. **It's logical** that we should study English every day.

(1) Without question   (2) It stands to reason
(3) As a rule

h. After the accident, the police officer **did what was necessary to** assist the injured man.

(1) took steps   (2) sized up   (3) put two and two together

Lesson 4: Agreement and Disagreement

Interview

The *Big W* supermarkets have opened delicatessens in most of their stores. Each delicatessen has its own manager. The local manager is Loretta Johnson. Her "deli" was opened six months ago. Since Loretta has become manager, her deli is the most successful of all *Big W* delicatessens.

The interviewer talked with Loretta about how she works with other people in the *Big W*.

Loretta: Oh, I enjoy being manager of the deli. **I'm on good terms** with everyone.

Interviewer: Yes, I know. But what about higher-level managers? Do you generally agree or disagree with them?

Loretta: Usually we **see eye to eye** on almost everything. When there is some question, the store manager usually **sides with** me. His name is Don Cromer. You know him, don't you?

Interviewer: Oh, yes. I'm just curious about how you two work together.

Loretta: As I said, we agree on almost everything. When we don't agree, he **gives it to me straight.**

Interviewer: Isn't that pretty harsh?

Loretta: No, no. He **doesn't bite my head off** or anything like that! He simply tells me the facts as he sees them. As a manager, I have to **be in line with** company policy. Other than that, Don **gives me a free hand.**

Interviewer: I see. Well, what about customers? Some people around here are very particular about their food.

Loretta: That's the truth! I can't complain, though. My customers are quite satisfied. Our policy is that the customer is always right. We always **give the customer the benefit of the doubt.**

Interviewer: How about your employees? Are they easy to manage?

Loretta: Yes, certainly. I believe in teamwork and coopera- tion. Oh, occasionally I have workers who **find fault with** everything. Usually they're the type who like to **pick quarrels with** their co-workers.

Interviewer: What do you do in that case?

Loretta: Well, I sit down with the person and discuss the problem. I simply **lay my cards on the table.** I explain that a team player is someone **after my own heart.** I want employees I can **go to bat for.** I will not work with any other kind of person.

Interviewer: What do you do next?

Loretta: I just ask the employee directly, **"Are you with me?"**

After (one's) own heart *to like someone because of common interests*

Diane and I both love tennis. She's a woman **after my own heart.**

Are you with me? *an expression meaning "Do you follow what I'm saying?"*

This is the last time I'll tolerate this kind of behavior. **Are you with me?**

Be in line with   *in agreement with*

All of the rules must **be in line with** company policy.

Be on good terms with   *to have friendly relations with*

Let Corey talk to the teacher for you. He**'s on good terms with her.**

Bite (one's) head off   *to answer someone angrily*

Heavens! All I said was "hello," and George almost **bit my head off!** He certainly is in a horrible mood!

Find fault with   *to criticize*

I don't care for Mike Parkman's attitude. He **finds fault with** practically everyone.

Give it to (someone) straight   *to criticize, to tell clearly, to speak honestly*

Don't make a big speech about how sorry you are. Just **give it to me straight.**

Give (one) a free hand   *to allow someone freedom of choice, to allow complete choice of action*

If you want Juanita to do a good job, you must **give her a free hand.**

Give (one) the benefit of the doubt   *to assume a person is innocent rather than guilty*

Maybe Bill did, and maybe he didn't do it. I'm **giving him the benefit of the doubt.**

Go to bat for (someone)   *to defend, to help someone*

I got the job because my previous employer was willing to go to **bat for** me. From now on when someone needs help, I'll **go to bat for him or her.**

Lay (one's) cards on the table   *to reveal all the facts, to be absolutely truthful*

I asked the salesman to tell me everything. He did so. He **laid his cards on the table,** telling me both the advantages and disadvantages of his product.

Pick a quarrel   *to seek the opportunity to argue or fight*

Don't pick a quarrel with your father. You'll just feel bad about it later.

See eye to eye   *to be in agreement*

Your mother and I **see eye to eye** about your taking the family car to New York. We both agree that it is not a good idea.

Side with (someone)   *to favor, to stand up for someone (to go to bat for)*

Margot and I see eye to eye on this question. I'm afraid I must **side with** her when it comes to a vote.

Exercise

Make up two short stories for the four scenes given below. Use the idioms under the pictures.

give someone a free hand, be in line with, side with

see eye to eye, go to bat for, after one's own heart

lay one's cards on the table, give someone the benefit of the doubt, be on good terms with

find fault with, bite someone's head off, give it to someone straight

35

Lesson 1: The Telephone; On the Phone

Interview

Larry Wong is the head of an office supplies company. Because of the need for daily contact with his salespeople and local businesses, Larry uses the telephone a lot.

The interviewer is calling Mr. Wong at Wong Office Supplies, Inc.

Receptionist: Good morning. Wong Office Supplies. May I help you?

Int: Good morning. This is Mr. Setzler. May I speak to Mr. Wong?

Receptionist: Mr. Wong is **tied up** on another line. Could I **put** you **on hold** for a minute?

Int: Yes. That'll be fine.

Receptionist: Thank you.

Larry: Good morning. What can I do for you?

Int: I'm calling about the telephone survey I am conducting. Remember? I spoke to you about it the other day.

Larry: **Of course.** You wanted to know how many **calls** I **make** a day. I told you I would check with my secretary. Let's see. She said I make about twenty calls a day. I have seven salespeople that I must contact everyday. Also, I have.... Excuse me. I have someone **on the other line.** Let me **put you in touch with** my secretary. She has all the information. Or, if you like, you can **call** me **back.**

Int: **Never mind,** Mr. Wong. I have most of what I need. I can **get in touch with** you, if I need to. Don't worry, you'll **hear from** me again.

Larry: **Call** me **up** any time. Or you can **drop** me **a line.**

Be tied up   *to be very busy*

I'm sorry I can't come this evening. **I'm tied up** at the office.

Call (someone) back   *to return a telephone call*

Hello, Bill? This is Susanna. My secretary left a message **to call** you **back.**

Call up   *to call someone by telephone*

I have to **call up** my dentist for an appointment. I have to **call** him **up** immediately because my tooth hurts.

Drop (someone) a line   *to write someone a brief letter or note*

I haven't written to my sister in over a week. I'd better **drop her a line** today.

Get in touch with   *to connect (usually by telephone or correspondence)*

Please **get in touch with** me about the exam sometime this week.

Hear from   *to receive a letter or telephone call from someone*

Have you **heard from** your friend in Spain lately?

37

Keep (someone) waiting   *to delay a meeting or contact with someone*

Hurry and finish your work! Don't **keep** your boss **waiting!**

Make a call   *to telephone, to use the telephone*

Excuse me. May I use your telephone? I have to **make a call.**

Never mind   *forget it, pay no attention to it, it is of no consequence*

Never mind! I'll do it myself.

Of course   *certainly, definitely*

Of course you can speak English.

On the phone (on the line) *to talk by telephone, to be using the telephone*

Elena is talking **on the phone** right now. She is **on the line** with her husband.

Put (someone) in touch with   *to connect someone with someone else*

The operator **put me in touch with** the head of the company.

Put (someone) on hold   *to have someone wait during a telephone call*

The secretary **put me on hold** while she looked for the papers I needed.

Put (someone) through (to) *to connect someone with someone else by telephone*

Operator, can you **put me through** to New York?

Exercises

1. Put the correct idiom in the following sentences.

Idioms

hear from   on the phone
make a call   call back
never mind

Sentences

a. I get nervous when I am talking _____ in English.

b. Bob wants me to _____ him _____ .

c. _____ , Maria. Just forget about it.

d. This is a pay phone. You need a quarter to _____ .

e. Do you _____ your sister often?

2. **Fill in the blanks with the following idioms.**

keep waiting   on the phone
get in touch with   put on hold
put through to   of course

Quiet, please, I'm _____ . I've tried for an hour
to _____ my wife. It's hard to hear because it's
a long distance call....Oh, operator? Would you_____me
_____ Susan Parkman in Columbia, South Carolina?
The number is (803) 276-6910. _____ , I'll wait
....Darn, she _____ me _____ . Sometimes I think
telephone operators like to _____ people _____ .

3. **Complete each sentence by selecting the correct idiom.**

a. I'm sorry Bill, but I have to stay at the office because

_____ .

(1) I'm tied up this morning   (2) my brother dropped me
a line   (3) Rachael called me up

b. Since you like to write letters, why don't you _____
_____ ?

(1) put me in touch with her   (2) drop her a line
(3) call her up

c. You can find out right now, if you _____ .

(1) call her up   (2) are tied up   (3) drop her a line

d. _____ Mr. Jones. I need to speak to him.

(1) Drop me a line   (2) Tie me up with
(3) Put me in touch with

39

Lesson 2: The Library

Interview

Emily Neal is the head librarian of the Community Library. She received her master's degree in Library Science in 1957.

Int: Good morning, Mrs. Neal. Oh, I see you're busy. I'll come back later.

Mrs. Neal: No, no. I'm glad you **came in.** I got your letter yesterday. I have **put together** most of the information you wanted. Here it is.

Int: Thank you very much.

Mrs. Neal: There is one problem. As I **looked over** your questions, I **ran across** one I couldn't **make out.** It **had** something **to do with** the types of people who use the library, I believe.

Int: Yes, I wanted to know what kinds of people use the library, such as young or old, students or business-people, men or women....

Mrs. Neal: Oh, all kinds of people use the library. At lunchtime you'll find mostly adults who come in to **read over** the newspapers and periodicals. After school, students come in to **look up** information for their school assignments. People say that because of television, most of us never **crack a book** anymore. But I find that fiction is as popular as ever.

Int: I see.

Mrs. Neal: Taste in books changes, but people still love to read. **By the way,** do you have a library card...?

Int: A library card? I'm afraid I don't have one. What do I have to **go through** to get one?

Mrs. Neal: It's no problem. Here's the form. **Fill in** your name, address, and phone number. You can **fill** it **out** now or take it home and **bring** it **back** anytime. **Read over** the library rules on the back of the form.

Int: Thank you, Mrs. Neal. You have been a big help.

Bring back   *to return something*

You didn't **bring back** the book you borrowed from me. Please **bring** it **back** today.

By the way   *incidentally*

By the way, your husband told me that his mother is coming for a visit.

Crack a book   *to read, to study*

If you don't **crack a book,** you'll never pass the exam.

Come in   *to enter*

Won't you **come in** and have a cup of coffee?

Fill in   *to complete (said of something missing or left blank)*

In the exercise section of this lesson **fill in** the blanks with the idiom. **Fill** them **in** correctly.

Fill out   *to complete (said of forms, applications, and so on)*

Everyone must **fill out** several forms to obtain a
passport. **Fill** them **out** carefully.

Go through   *to endure, to experience, to undergo*

Parents **go through** a lot to educate their children.

Have to do with   *pertaining to*

I believe her job **has to do with** Customs Import Laws.

Look over   *to examine, to inspect*

I always **look over** my homework before I turn it in. You should
look yours **over** too.

Look up   *to consult a reference book for, to search for*

I need to **look up** her number in the telephone book. I **looked** it **up**
last week but I forgot it.

Make out   *to identify, to distinguish, to decipher*

In the dark, Carol couldn't **make out** who was coming toward her.
She couldn't **make** anything **out.**

Put together   *to assemble*

This kite was easy to **put together.** My mother helped me **put** it
together.

Read over   *to read hurriedly, to scan*

Please **read over** my notes before the meeting. **Read** them **over**
quickly.

Run across   *to encounter, to find unexpectedly*

Mother **ran across** some old snapshots of us.

Exercises

1. **Read the paragraph. Replace the boldface verbs and phrases with the correct idiom from the list.**

by the way   ran across
put together   came in
filled in   looked them over
cracked a book   make out

Bob couldn't get a job. He couldn't read well. In fact, he never **read.** I tried to help him get a job. When he **entered** the Employment Office, he couldn't **decipher** the job application form. I had to help him **assemble** the correct information. After he **completed** the forms, I **examined** them. He applied for a job as a clerk in an insurance company. He got the job! He worked hard and went to night school. That was five years ago. **Incidentally,** I **encountered** Bob last week. Now he is a vice-president in charge of sales.

2. **Fill in or select the correct idiom.**

a. "_____ your name here, please."

   (1) fill in   (2) fill out   (3) make out

b. When you take books out of the library, don't forget to _____ .

   (1) fill them out   (2) bring them back
   (3) put them together

c. Before you sign your name, _____ the card.
   (1) run across   (2) look up   (3) read over

d. To get a good job you have to _____ a lot.
   (1) go through   (2) make out   (3) bring back

e. I hate filling out forms. What does that _____ my job?
   (1) come in   (2) have to do with   (3) run across

43

3. Fill out the following forms:

```
┌─────────────────────────────────────────────┐
│              LIBRARY CARD                    │
│  Name: _____         │
│     The bearer of this card is entitled to all of │
│  the rights and privileges of the           │
│          COMMUNITY LIBRARY                   │
└─────────────────────────────────────────────┘
┌─────────────────────────────────────────────┐
│              JOB APPLICATION                 │
│  Name: _____         │
│  Address: _____         │
│           _____         │
│                                              │
│  Previous Employment                         │
│       1. _____          │
│       2. _____          │
│       3. _____          │
│  Education                                   │
│          _____          │
│          _____          │
│          _____          │
└─────────────────────────────────────────────┘
```

Lesson 3: Directions (Travel)

Interview

The interviewer pretended he was lost. He asked a businessman on the street how to return to the Yates Building. The man was very helpful. He even gave the interviewer a ride to the Yates Building.

Int: Excuse me, sir. I'm lost. Can you tell me how to find the Yates Building? I've been **looking all over for** it.

Man: I'll **do my best. First of all,** you **had better turn around.** Then you'll have to **go up to** that corner over there.

Int: That one?

Man: Yes, that one. Then turn left. **Before long,** you'll come to a big hill. **At the foot of** the hill is a large museum. The Yates Building is **next to** the museum.

45

Int: Yes, now I remember. Thank you very much. I **had better** hurry or I won't **get back** in time for my appointment. I didn't realize the Yates Building was so **far away.**

Man: I **live on** a street near there and I'm **on my way home.** Would you like a ride?

Int: Yes, **thanks a lot!**

At the foot of   *at the base of something (hill, statue, bed, mountain, and so on)*

She kept a blanket **at the foot of** her bed.

Before long   *soon, after a short period of time*

Before long, it will be Christmas.

Do one's best   *to use one's maximum ability*

You should **do your best** in school.

Far away   *at a great distance*

The stars are far, **far away.**

First of all   *to begin with, the first of a series of things*

First of all, we'll discuss business, then we'll eat lunch, and finally, we'll play a round of golf.

Get back   *to return*

I want to **get back** home by five o'clock.

Go up to   *to approach, to get close to*

The student was afraid to **go up to** the teacher and ask for help.

Had better   *ought to, should*

You **had better** wear your raincoat. It's raining.

Live on   *to dwell on a street, avenue, and so on*

I live on Beech Street.

Look all over (for)   *to search everywhere (for)*

The child **looked all over** the house **for** her lost doll.

Next to   *beside, close to*

I sat **next to** my father at the baseball game.

On one's way   *in the process of going home, to work, and so on*

On her way home, the woman met an old friend.

Thanks a lot   *thank you very much*

Thanks a lot for the homemade candy.

Turn around   *to turn and face in the opposite direction, to turn 180 degrees*

Turn around and look in the mirror.

Exercises

1. **Read the sentence with each substitution.**

   a. The little boy is standing **at the foot of**   the bed.
   the stairs.
   the hill.
   the mountain.

   b. **First of all,**   we must do our homework.
   I want to make a phone call.
   you should get a job.
   John should get in touch with me.
   she must study harder.

   c. **I live on**   very little money.
   a large salary.
   Harper Street.
   the beach.
   an island.

47

d. Eric is standing **next to** me.
the door.
the television.
you.
Carlos and Keiko.

e. **Before long,** I'll be twenty years old.
Dad will be home from work.
you'll like English.
our new house will be finished.

f. **On my way home,** I ate an apple.
I saw a dog chase a cat.
I stopped for a newspaper.
I fell in a ditch.
I bought a bottle of milk.

g. You **had better** finish your work.
eat your lunch.
go to the doctor.
do your best.
turn around.

2. **Read the paragraph. Replace the boldface words with the correct idiom from the list.**

get back	first of all
look all over for	do your best
far away	go up to

Success often seems to be **at a great distance** but if you **use your maximum ability,** you cannot fail. **To begin with,** you ought to **return** to the basic skills—reading, writing, and arithmetic. Then you should **search everywhere for** what interests you! When you find out what you want, **approach** it as you would a friend!

Lesson 4: Requests for Directions (How to)

Interview

Kay Durham is a supervisor at Data Electronics. Today she is teaching a new employee, Bill Wheat, to operate one of the duplicating machines.

Int: Do you always have to teach new employees to run the machines, Kay?

Kay: Usually not. **From time to time,** I do. This is our new model, and I am the only one in the office trained to run it.

Bill: Well, I **give up.** I've tried it **again and again** and I can't get it right.

Kay: Okay, Bill, let's **find out** what you are doing wrong.

Bill: Well, I **turn on** the machine like this. Then I put in the pages like this, **one after another.** See, the copies keep coming out fuzzy.

Kay: I see. That is a problem. I need to work on this machine. **Turn off** the power and let's go to lunch. We can **go into** this problem this afternoon.

Bill: How do you **turn it off?**

Int: Well, Bill, you've **worked on** this machine all day. Do you still want to give up?

Bill: No, **to my surprise,** it was easier **after a while.** Kay gives good directions.

Int: Before long, you'll **be good at** it, too.

Bill: Yes, I think so, too. Maybe Kay will also show me how to get a raise.

Again and again   *repeatedly*

My teacher has helped me **again and again.**

49

After a while   *later, after a short period of time*

After a while, English becomes easier.

Be good at   *to excel at something, to show high ability for*

She **is good at** solving problems.

Find out   *to learn, to discover*

Find out how to apply for a job as an English teacher. You can **find it out** at the board of eduction.

From time to time   *occasionally*

From time to time, I go back to my hometown.

Give up   *to stop trying, to abandon, to quit*

No, Edward did not **give up** smoking. He wanted to **give** it **up,** but he couldn't.

Go into   *to discuss, to consider*

Next week in class we shall **go into** idioms in American speech.

One after another   *in sequence, in a series*

The boss gave me many tasks **one after another.**

To (one's) surprise   *unexpectedly, surprisingly*

To my surprise, he's doing well.

Turn off   *to disconnect, to terminate, to shut off*

Turn off the lights before you go to bed. **Turn** them **off** in all the rooms.

Turn on   *to start, to connect*

Turn on the power by pushing the red button.
Turn it off before you leave.

Work on   *to attempt to solve, to fix, to complete*

Let's **work on** our homework.

50

Exercise

Use the idioms. Tell a short story about each picture.

turn on, turn off, again and
again

_____

_____

_____

give up, one after another,
after awhile

_____

_____

_____

to one's surprise, be good at,
work on

_____

_____

_____

from time to time, find out, go
into

_____

_____

_____

51

Lesson 1: Asking for Help

Interview

Mrs. Vega is a neighbor of Pete Martin, a fireman. She has a white kitten named Snowy. The interviewer was talking with Peter Martin, when Mrs. Vega came running up to Pete. Her kitten was up in a big oak tree. The kitten was afraid to climb down.

Mrs. Vega: Pete! I'm so glad you're home! Could you **give me a hand?** Snowy is up in the tree and can't get down.

Pete: I'd be glad to **lend a hand.** Just a minute and I'll get my ladder.

Mrs. Vega: It's so nice of you to **help out.**

Pete: Come on, Hugh. You can **help** me **out,** too.

Int.: Okay.

Pete: Snowy is really way up there, almost at the top.

Int.: Shall I climb up with you?

Pete: No, **I'm used to** heights. You might fall and **kill yourself.**

Int.: Okay.

Be used to *to be accustomed to*

He **isn't used to** asking for help.

Give (someone) a hand *to help (someone)*

I'm ready to **give you a hand,** if you need it.

Help out *to assist*

Jean would like to **help out** at the hospital. She **helps** me **out** a lot.

Kill oneself *to commit suicide (often used as an exaggeration for "to hurt oneself")*

Don't **kill yourself** with overwork.

Lend (someone) a hand *to help, to give assistance*

Good neighbors always **lend a hand** in a crisis.

Interview

Peter climbs up the oak tree to rescue Snowy.

Mrs. Vega: **Take it easy,** Pete. **Look out for** those branches! Please, be careful.

Pete: Yes, Ma'am. I can handle it. . . .Ouch!

Mrs. Vega: Poor Snowy. I can hear her **crying out for** help.

Pete: Don't worry, I can. . . .Ouch! Don't scratch, Snowy. **Take it easy,** Snowy.

Mrs. Vega: I'm so glad you were **on hand,** Pete.

Pete: Well, here you are, Mrs. Vega. Here's Snowy, safe and sound.

Mrs. Vega: Thanks, Pete. But those scratches look pretty bad.

Pete: Not really, but I'll never **take part in** an animal rescue again.

Mrs. Vega: Oh?

Pete: I have to tell you something, Mrs. Vega. I hate cats!

Cry out for   *to call for (with a sense of urgency)*

If you're in trouble, just **cry out for** help. I'll come right away.

Look out for   *to be alert for, to be on the alert for, to watch out for*

Look out for cars when crossing the street.

On hand   *present, accessible, available, in attendance*

Always keep your dictionary **on hand.**

Take it easy   *stay calm, be calm, slow down*

Don't worry. I'm going to help you. Just **take it easy.**

Take part in   *to participate in*

The fireman **took part in** a daring rescue.

Exercise

Tell about the rescue of Snowy in your own words. Use some of these idioms: **be used to, give (someone) a hand, help out, kill oneself, lend (someone) a hand, cry out for, look out for, on hand, take it easy,** and **take part in.**

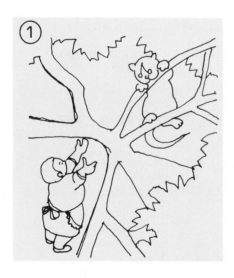 

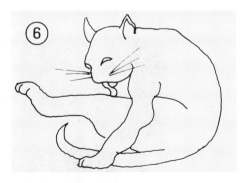

Lesson 2: Decisions

Interview

George Taylor, Frank Brunetti, and Alice Young are senior managers at Bond Textile Company. They meet each Friday to discuss company problems.

Int: Thank you all for allowing me to sit in on this meeting. Frank, what problems are you **working out** these days?

Frank: I **was absent from** last week's meeting, so I'm not sure. We had been talking about **a number of** things.

Alice: Basically, we were trying to **think up** ways to **cut down** on production cost by **making the best use of** our new cutting machines.

Int: Do you feel that these meetings are useful?

George: Yes, definitely. We've been able to **bring about** some important changes. **For example,** last month our problem was safety procedures for the cutting machines. We solved that problem by **working out** safety standards for all equipment, not just for cutting machines.

56

Frank: Those were some meetings! They went **on and on,** but **at the end of** those meetings we had a very good set of standards.

Alice: We're very **proud of** those standards. Without these meetings we would never have **gotten the idea for** those safety standards. None of our competitors can **come up to** our new safety record.

A number of   *several*

A number of decisions must be made every day.

At the end of   *at the terminal point, at the close of, at the finish of*

At the end of the meeting, Frank read through the list of accomplishments.

Be absent from   *to be missing, not present*

When I had the flu, I **was absent from** school for one week.

Be proud of   *to take pride in, to feel good about*

I'm **very proud of** my son's decision to be a doctor.

Bring about   *to cause, to cause to happen*

Our meeting **brought about** a change in company policy. We **brought** it **about** unanimously.

Come up to   *to get close to, to approach closely, to meet*

Michelle tried hard to **come up** to the teacher's standards.

Cut down on   *to reduce*

Robert wants to **cut down on** candy and desserts.

For example   *used to introduce an example*

A fish can be cooked many ways. **For example,** you can broil it, bake it, or fry it.

Get the idea for   *to conceive, to come up with*

Where did you **get the idea for** this poem?

Make the best use (of) *to use to maximum ability, to take advantage of something to the greatest degree*

He can **make the best use of** his teaching experience on his new job at the university.

On and on   *continuously, continually*

The teacher talked **on and on** about popular idioms.

Think up   *to invent, to discover, to devise*

The boy tried to **think up** an excuse for being late. He couldn't **think** one **up.**

Work out   *to develop, to solve, to plan*

We were able to **work out** all the details for our vacation. We **worked** them out last week.

Exercises

1. Read the sentences.

    a. He made **a number of** decisions.
       John discovered **a number of** problems.
       Sue had **a number of** friends.
       Data Corporation has developed **a number of** new products.
       Education gives us **a number of** new opportunities.

    b. We get paid **at the end of** the week.
       I'm tired **at the end of** the day.
       The car stopped **at the end of** the road.
       The report will be ready **at the end of** the month.
       We left **at the end of** the movie.

    c. Problems and decisions are part of our lives.
       For example, with very little money you must spend wisely.
       For example, every day we must choose between right and wrong.
       You must, **for example,** decide what to wear every day.

You must decide, **for example,** what to eat every day.
For example, you alone must decide who you are.

d. How did she **get the idea for** that new book?
Where did you **get the idea for** a camping trip?

e. It rained **on and on** for days.
The baby cried **on and on** all night long.
On and on, the long road led to the sea.

f. **Make the best use of** your mind.
Make the best use of your ability.
Make the best use of your money.
Make the best use of your time.

2. **Write a definition for each idiom.**

a. That man did not **come up to** me. _____

b. Frank **was absent from** the last meeting. _____

c. Meetings often **bring about** changes. _____

d. Let's **work out** the answers to these problems. _____

e. Let's **cut down on** waste! _____

f. Alice **thinks up** great ideas. _____

g. I'm **proud of** your progress in English. _____

Lesson 3: Aches and Pains

Interview

Jean Davis is a doctor at a large university. She runs the health clinic there. She sees fifteen to twenty students each day. Right now she is examining Jerry Moran, a young man with an injured foot.

Int: Do you mind, Doctor, if I watch what you're doing?

Dr. Davis: No, I don't mind. Jerry, **pull up** your pants leg and **take off** your shoe and sock. I'll have to **wash off** your foot.

Int: How did you hurt your foot, Jerry?

Jerry: I was **playing catch** with a friend and stepped on some broken glass.

Dr. Davis: I'm **all through with** your bandage now, Jerry. I think you can **take care of** it by yourself, but **come back** in three days anyway. I would like to check your foot then.

Jerry: Right, Dr. Davis. Thanks a lot.

Be all through with   *completed, finished*

I'm **all through with** school for today.

Come back   *to return*

Soon after I left the dentist, the pain **came back.**

Play catch   *to toss (throw) a ball back and forth*

When I **play catch** with my father, the baseball hurts my hand.

Pull up   *to raise, to pull upwards*

Pull up your shirt sleeve and the nurse will clean the wound. **Pull** it **up** higher, please.

Take care of   *to assume charge of, to protect, to watch over*

After school, Tom helps his mother **take care of** his baby sister.

Take off   *to remove*

The Japanese **take off** their shoes when they come into the house. They always **take** them **off** in the house.

Wash off   *to cleanse*

After she played football, she had to **wash off** the dirt. She **washed** it **off** in the shower.

Interview

The interviewer continues his conversation with Dr. Davis.

Int: With so many students at the university, you must have a number of different problems.

Dr. Davis: Yes, I have to be able to handle any problems that come up. Usually students **get sick** with the flu or some virus. In the winter, students **catch colds** a lot. There is always **something the matter.** We see them all here in the clinic.

Int: What do you do if the student is really ill?

Dr. Davis: As I said, most of the students have minor problems. They **get well** right away with a minimum of care. If

61

        students **get worse,** we put them in the university hospital.

Int: You seem to enjoy working with these young people.

Dr. Davis: I really do. We get to know **one another** very well. Even after graduation, a number of them come back for a visit.

Catch (a) cold   *to contract a cold, to become ill with a cold*

Many people **catch cold** in the winter.
I **caught a cold** last week.

Get sick   *to become ill*

I hope that I don't **get sick** on the airplane.

Get well   *to become better, to become healthy*

Bob is sick. I hope he **gets well** soon.

Get worse   *to become more ill, to decline in health, to worsen in condition*

My headache **got worse** as the traffic **got worse.**

One another   *each other, between two or more people*

Gina and Mario like each other, but Ari and Nancy love **one another.**

Something the matter (with) *something wrong (with)*

This car has **something the matter** with the engine.

Exercise

Make up a short story for each picture using the idioms.

catch a cold, get worse, get well

_____
_____
_____
_____
_____
_____

62

pull up, wash off, take care of, all through with

_____

_____

_____

_____

_____

_____

play catch, one another, take off

_____

_____

_____

_____

_____

something the matter (with), get sick, come back

_____

_____

_____

_____

_____

63

Lesson 4: The Unexpected

Interview

Pete Martin is a fireman. He received an award for bravery last week.

Int: Pete, would you mind telling me how you got the award for bravery?

Pete: It's a funny story. Every day on my way home I **go by** the Master Pet Store. I like to look in the window at new puppies. I've been thinking about buying a bird dog for the family.

Int: Is that when you saw the store **catch fire?**

Pete: No, I didn't see it **catch fire.** The fire had already started. **In a moment,** however, it **turned into** a large blaze.

Int: What did you do then?

Pete: Well, it was hard to **get into** the store. The heat was awful! I had to **turn back** twice because of the smoke. The dogs were barking and running around like crazy!

I was **in and out** of the store about ten times. The heat was bad, but I just had to **let** those animals **out**.

Int: Did you get them all out?

Pete: Oh, yes. But when the animals were outside, they **ran away.** I thought the puppies were going to **die of** fright. It took the whole fire department more than two hours to **bring** all those animals **back.**

Int: It took courage to do what you did.

Pete: Not really. It took more courage to get Mrs. Vega's cat down from that oak tree. I tell you, as a fireman you never know what's going to **come up!**

Bring (something) back   *to return (something)*

You can't **bring back** the past. No, you can't **bring** it **back.**

Catch fire   *to ignite, to start to burn*

Trees **catch fire** when lightning strikes them.

Come up (with)   *to arise, to develop, to discover, to find*

Unexpected problems **come up** every day. We must **come up with** new solutions.

Die of   *to cause death from*

When I failed my test, I thought I would **die of** shame.

Get into   *to enter, to gain access to, to be admitted*

It was hard to **get into** this university.

Go by   *to pass, to move along*

She becomes smarter as time **goes by.**

In a moment   *in a very short period of time, momentarily*

In a moment, I'll have the answer to this problem.

In and out   *to enter and exit repeatedly*

I **was in and out** of the office all day.

Let out *to free, to set free, to release*

The teacher **let out** the class ten minutes early. She **let** us **out** only because tomorrow is a holiday.

Run away *to flee, to escape*

She tried to **run away** from the thief.

Turn back *to return, to retrace one's steps*

The road was so dangerous we **turned back.**

Turn into *to become*

It may **turn into** a sunny day after all.

1. **Replace the boldface words with the idiom in parentheses for each sentence.**

    a. Difficult problems often **become** easy problems. (turn into)

    b. When the house **ignited,** everyone ran across the street. (catch fire)

    c. It's hard to **be admitted into** this school. (get into)

    d. Don't **flee** from your problems. Face them. (run away)

    e. **Shortly,** I shall find out the answer. (in a moment)

    f. Everyday my boss **conceives of** a new idea. (come up with)

2. **Read the sentence with each substitution.**

    a. Dolores thought she **would die of** fright.
    starvation.
    shame.
    boredom.
    embarrassment.

    b. They were   **in and out** of the house all day.
    George goes
    I'll be
    He was
    Ed is

66

c. Don't forget to **bring back** the library books.
the sweater you borrowed.
the money you owe me.
my umbrella.
your job application form.

d. My wife **let out** a scream.
the cat.
a deep breath.
the news that I lost my job.

e. Did you **go by** the pet store?
my house on the way to work?
the store on the corner?
that town on the way to the mountain?

f. Carolyn **turned back** because of bad weather.
because of rough roads.
because she was frightened.
because her mother was calling her.

Lesson 1: Loving People And Wanting Things

Interview

The interviewer talked with two teenagers, Brian and Elizabeth, about love, friendship, and the kinds of things they would like to have.

Interviewer: What can you tell me about modern romance.

Elizabeth: Nothing. I mean I don't know. You should ask Bobby and Linda. Bobby **has a crush on** Linda. They've only been dating for two months, but he's really in love. Linda really **got under his skin.**

Brian: Well, Linda's fallen **head over heels** in love with Bobby, too. He practically **swept her off her feet.**

Interviewer: What do young people like to do these days?

Elizabeth: I don't know. I guess it's the same everywhere. I **get a kick out of** roller skating. And **I'm nuts about** roller disco.

Brian: How true. That's all she wants to do—just skate at the roller disco.

Interviewer: Don't you like to dance, Brian?

Brian: Oh, sure. I **get a kick out of** it. I love the music and the crowds. But I'm not a fanatic about disco like Elizabeth.

Elizabeth: I guess I **am crazy about** it. **I have my heart set on** a new pair of skates for my birthday. I want a new disco outfit, too. Then I want to dance **to my heart's content**.

Interviewer: And what do you want, Brian?

Brian: **I want out.**

Interviewer: Do you mean you want to break up with Elizabeth?

Brian: No, I was only joking. **I'm just not as crazy about** roller disco as Elizabeth.

Elizabeth: Brian's always joking. We **go steady** just **for laughs**. With Bobby and Linda it's **no laughing matter**. They are serious about each other.

Be crazy about   *to be enthusiastic about, to like enormously*

I'm just crazy about Barbara. I really love her.

Be nuts about   *to be enthusiastic about, to like enormously*

If you**'re nuts about** Barbara, you should ask her for a date.

For laughs   *for fun, for pleasure*

Why are you so serious all the time? Don't you ever do anything just **for laughs?**

Get a kick out of   *to enjoy very much*

I **get a** real **kick out of** growing my own tomatoes in the summer.

Get under (one's) skin *to irritate, annoy; to bother (in the sense of to love or to think about all the time)*

Alice has really **gotten under my skin.** I think I'm in love with her.

Go steady   *to date only one person*

Well, look at that! Carla and Eduardo **are going steady.**

69

Have a crush on   *to be very fond of, to be in love with*

Lee has always **had a crush on** Lucy.

Have (one's) heart set on   *to desire greatly*

I'm sorry John didn't get that new car. He **had his heart set on** it.

Head over heels   *completely, enthusiastically*

Joe fell **head over heels** in love with Suzanne.

No laughing matter   *something not to be treated lightly*

Failing your English test is **no laughing matter.**

Sweep (one) off   *to overwhelm someone with one's power, skill,*
(one's) feet   *looks, personality, and so on.*

John's shy smile and gentle manners literally **swept Ellen off her feet.** In fact, she fell head over heels in love with him.

To (one's) heart's content   *to one's complete satisfaction*

Last week we had a seafood dinner. We ate boiled lobster **to our heart's content.**

Want out   *to desire to break an association with an enterprise or person*

Jean liked this hunting trip when we first started. After three days in the woods, she **wanted out.**

Exercise

Make sentences using the idioms in parentheses to complete the paragraphs.

a. Mary said that Mike and Sue are getting a divorce. George responded, "That's impossible. _____ ." (be crazy about)

b. Fernando plays tennis every day. I asked him why he played tennis so much. Fernando replied, " _____ ." (be nuts about)

70

c. Aki complained about going to the mountains for the weekend. "It costs too much. It's too cold. Why should we do it?" Yuko replied, " _____ ." (for laughs)

d. Aki thought again about going to the mountains. Yuko was laughing about how seriously he thought about it. Aki said, " _____ ." (no laughing matter)

e. After the weekend in the mountains, Aki was happy and relaxed. "You know," he said, " _____ ." (get a kick out of)

f. The children had to play in the house all day. It was raining outside. Their mother said, " _____ ." (get under my skin)

g. John and Marie were holding hands in the park. George saw them and smiled. He said to himself, " _____ ." (have a crush on)

h. Betty ran up to George. "Have you heard about John and Marie?" she asked. George said, " _____ ." (go steady)

i. Betty smiled when she thought about John and Marie. "I wish," she said, " _____ ." (head over heels)

j. Ed wanted to go to an Italian restaurant. "Come on, Mary," he said, " _____ ." (have my heart set on)

k. Jo Ann is so lovely and charming. "I love her smile," said Roger. " _____ ." (sweep me off my feet)

l. Three women decided to have a party. The plans got more and more elaborate. The first woman finally said, " _____ ." (want out)

m. At the restaurant Ed ate a large plate of spaghetti. He wanted more spaghetti, but he was worried about his diet. "Don't worry," Mary told him, " _____ ." (to your heart's content)

Lesson 2: Getting Angry and Keeping Cool

Interview

The interviewer continues to talk with a group of teenagers about feelings such as anger. The interviewer asks them how they control themselves and what they do to remain calm.

Marie: Well, that's easy. I know what makes me angry. Whenever I see my boyfriend with another girl, I **blow my top.** How do I control myself? I don't. When I'm angry, I can't **calm down.**

John: Yes, sir. That's the truth. When Marie **loses her temper** there's nothing you can do. I should know. I'm her boyfriend.

Interviewer: And how about you, Jimmy? How do you remain calm?

Jimmy: I don't like to get mad. I always **keep my cool.**

Sue Ann: Jimmy! How can you say that! Why, you **fly off the handle** at every little thing.

Jimmy: I do not! My father may **blow his stack** all the time, but I'm like my mother. She never **loses her grip.**

Sue Ann: Oh, come on, Jimmy. You're **going off half-cocked** right now. If you're like your mother, then **keep your grip!**

Jimmy: I guess you're right. I do **see red** occasionally.

Interviewer: What about you, Ted? You've been very quiet. How do you stay so calm?

Ted: Well, when I feel like I'm going to get angry, I usually run a mile or two. I like jogging and it's a good way to **blow off steam.** In today's world you have to **keep cool.**

Blow off steam   *to vent one's anger and, that way, gain relief*

When Harvey gets mad, he **blows off steam** by screaming at everyone.

Blow (one's) stack   *to become angry and lose control of oneself*

Oh, no! If Cherie finds out you spilled ink on her coat, she'**ll blow her stack.**

Blow (one's) top   *to become angry and lose control of oneself*

I knew it would happen! Cherie found out about her coat and she **blew her top.**

Calm down   *to gain control of oneself*

Later Cherie **calmed down** and apologized for her behavior.

Fly off the handle *to become angry very quickly, to lose control of oneself suddenly (to blow one's stack)*

When my father heard that I had wrecked the car, he **flew off the handle.**

Go off half-cocked *to act prematurely, to react without forethought*

Listen, Harry. This is a tense situation. Everyone is a little angry. This is no time **to go off half-cocked.**

Keep cool *to remain calm*

This was a dangerous storm. Lightning struck a nearby tree. Throughout the storm the whole family **kept cool.** I was proud of them.

Keep (one's) cool *to maintain one's calm attitude*

The angry crowd shouted and screamed at the police officer. Admirably, he **kept his cool.** Finally, he was able to calm everyone down.

Keep (one's) grip *to maintain one's control or ability*

Don't let all of your personal problems bother you so much. Don't let them affect your job. Try to **keep your grip.**

Lose (one's) grip *to lose one's control, to show signs of weakening*

Mary Jo's report is a mess. She's been late for work every morning this week. I think she's **losing her grip.**

Lose (one's) temper *to become very angry*

Every time Jorge doesn't get what he wants, he **loses his temper.**

See red *to become angry (to lose one's temper)*

I can't stand that guy. Every time he comes in the office, I **see red.**

Exercise

Study each picture. Select one idiom for each picture and make a statement that helps describe the picture.

74

_____ He's keeping his cool.

_____ He's blowing off steam.

_____ He's keeping his grip.

_____ He's not going off half-cocked.

_____ She's blowing her top.

_____ She's keeping cool.

_____ She has calmed down.

_____ She's seeing red.

75

Lesson 3: Worry and Hope

Interview—**Worry**

Mike Parkman runs a camp ground and recreation park. The camp ground is between two rivers that form a big lake. It is a great place for fishing, swimming, boating, and camping. However, because of the gas shortage and extremely hot weather, business is not so good.

Interviewer: How's business, Mike?

Mike: Business isn't so good. This gas shortage and gas prices have really hurt the recreational business in general. People are just staying home. Now it's this weather! I tell you, it's **driving me to drink.**

Interviewer: It's really that bad, Mike?

Mike: It's really that bad. I didn't **sleep a wink** last night. I'm worried **to death.**

Interviewer: Worrying won't help. You've got to take it easy or you'll **crack up.**

Mike: You're right. **I'll go nuts,** if I keep worrying the way I do. My wife Susan complains that **I'm on edge** all the time. She told me **not to cry over spilled milk.**

Interviewer: I think she's right. You have to quit worrying and plan for the future.

Mike: I know, I know. But this thing **preys on my mind** all the time. I don't know what to do.

Be on edge   *to be nervous, irritable*

Excuse me for getting angry, **I'm** just **on edge** today.

Crack up   *to have a mental breakdown*

If Mary Ann keeps worrying about school all the time, she'll **crack up.**

Cry over spilled milk   *to complain about something which can not be changed*

I know you had to work late and you missed the movie. Well, there's nothing you can do about it now. **Don't cry over spilled milk.**

Drive (one) to drink   *to irritate someone excessively*

That stupid fellow is going **to drive me to drink!**

Go nuts   *to become crazy*

If those children don't quit making so much noise, I'll **go nuts.**

Not to sleep a wink   *to stay awake, to lie in bed and not sleep*

I worried so much about the final exam I didn't **sleep a wink** last night.

Prey on (one's) mind   *to worry continuously*

The fact that I have to make a speech at my old high school next week constantly **preys on my mind.**

To death   *completely (to an extreme)*

I love my wife, but her job worries me **to death.** She's a professional sky diver.

Interview—Hope

This interview with Mike Parkman takes place two weeks after the first interview. The weather is good. Many families are now at Mike's camp ground.

Mike: I tell you this break in the weather is **a shot in the arm.** The camp is almost full this week. I'm **keeping my fingers crossed** that things will **turn out** all right.

Interviewer: That's great, Mike.

Mike: Susan told me to **take heart.** She said this bad spell couldn't last forever.

Interviewer: I suppose you're **looking forward to** a lot more business for the rest of the summer.

Mike: Oh, yes. I'm more optimistic now. Still, it feels funny to be **at the mercy of** the fish, the weather, and gas prices!

At the mercy of   *dependent upon, in the power of*

Farmers are always **at the mercy of** the weather.

Keep (one's) fingers crossed   *to hope, to hope that everything will turn out well*

I hope you get the scholarship you applied for. **I'll keep my fingers crossed** for you.

Look forward to   *to expect, anticipate*

The school year is almost over. I'm **looking forward to** the summer vacation.

Take heart   *to become encouraged*

Stop worrying and **take heart.** Things can't get worse.

Shot in the arm   *a stimulus of courage, enthusiasm, and so on*

I just heard that the state of the economy is starting to go up. That's just **the shot in the arm** we need.

Turn out *to become, to result*

I can't come to the party tonight. Please tell me tomorrow how it **turned out.**

Exercise 1

Replace the boldface words and phrases with the correct idiom in the proper form.

My job is very hard. It **is irritating me excessively.** If I don't quit working so hard, I'm going **to have a mental breakdown. I'm nervous** all the time. **I couldn't sleep** last night. I think I may **go crazy.** Oh, well, it is my job and I have to do it. There is no use in **complaining about what's done.** Yet it **does worry me.** In fact, I'm worried **completely!**

Exercise 2

Replace the boldface words and phrases with the correct idiom in the proper form.

Hooray! I got a raise. That was like **a stimulus of encouragement!** My job **has become** fine. I am no longer **dependent upon** my supervisor's ideas. Yes, it's time **to become encouraged.** I shall **hope for the best** and **anticipate** a better future.

Lesson 4: Fear and Courage

Interview — Fear

The interviewer talks with two students in the local community college. Both students are English majors. Their names are Amy Blake and Tom Roman.

Interviewer: Starting college can be a fearful experience. That's what I want to talk to you about. I'm curious about what frightens you about college life?

Amy: I'm afraid of arguments. I don't **have the heart** for confrontation. That's one thing I notice about college classrooms. More students will argue with the professor. It makes me nervous. I don't **have the stomach for** that.

Tom: I don't see it that way. I like intellectual debates. The professors like to be challenged occasionally. It **keeps them on their toes.**

Amy: Well, I suppose you're right. Teachers don't live **in fear of** ideas.

Interviewer: Do you debate with your English professor, Tom?

Tom: Once in a while, I do. Usually I **chicken out.** Professor Wilks is so smart that she can **make a monkey out of me.**

Amy: I don't blame you for **chickening out.** Many students have tried to debate her. She's so logical that they soon **lose heart.**

Chicken out   *to lose one's courage*

George almost went up to Linda and asked her to go to the dance, but he **chickened out.**

Have the heart (to)   *to have the courage (to)*

Poor Marion! I don't **have the heart** to tell her that she wasn't accepted for the job of editor of the school newspaper.

Have the stomach for   *to have the courage for, to be able to endure*

I like most sports, but I don't **have the stomach for** karate or boxing.

Keep on one's toes   *to insure that one remains alert and active*

My students' questions **keep me on my toes.**

Live in fear of   *to be continually afraid of*

Some people **live in fear of** losing their money and other worldly possessions.

Lose heart   *to become discouraged*

I tried and tried to learn to dance like the disco dancers. Now I have **lost heart.** I still can't dance.

Make a monkey out of (someone) *to ridicule, to outdo or surpass someone*

Jim did so much better in our tennis match that he **made a monkey out of** me.

Interview — Courage

The interviewer continues to talk with Amy and Tom. This time they discuss courage.

Interviewer: What is a courageous person as far as you're concerned?

Tom: I think a friend who will **stick up for** you is courageous. Also a courageous person is someone who will **take charge of** any situation. My roommate is a brave guy. He'll **wade into** any problem no matter how dangerous.

Amy: I think my father is courageous. He has courage because he **stands up for his beliefs.** My father **prides himself on standing up for** what he believes in.

Pride (oneself) on *to be proud of*

Donna **prides herself on** her business sense.

Stand up for *to support, to champion the cause of*

Every citizen must **stand up for** what he or she believes.

Stick up for *to defend*

My older brother **sticks up for** me when the older boys are picking on me.

Take charge of *to assume control or direction of*

Harley Davis is going to **take charge of** our office. His title will be office manager.

Wade into *to apply oneself diligently*

A hero is one who will **wade into** the most difficult and arduous tasks.

Exercise

Study each picture. Select one idiom for each picture and make a statement that helps describe the picture.

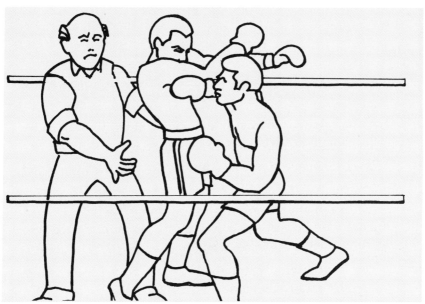

chicken out, in fear of, lose heart, keep someone on his/her toes

stand up for, stick up for

pride oneself on, take charge of, wade into

Lesson 1: Friendship

Interview

Leigh and Kate are both ten years old. They go to the same school. Leigh and Kate are "best friends."

Int: Kate, I want to ask you how you and Leigh met? How did you **make friends** with **each other?**

Kate: Well, last year at school some boys tried to **take away** my bike.

Leigh: And I **ran after** them and made them **give** it **back.** And Kate was so happy. She shared her lunch with me. We've been friends ever since.

Kate: Yes, that's what happened. That's why Leigh is my friend. I can **count on** her.

Leigh: I can **count on** Kate, too.

Int: What kinds of things do you both like to do?

Leigh: We like to **go for walks** a lot and talk about our friends. Sometimes Kate **comes home** with me after school and

we ride our skateboards. We just like to do things with **each other.**

Kate: And we like to **make up** stories about what we'll be doing when we **grow up**—like having parties and **going out** to restaurants and to the movies.

Int: Do you think you'll still be friends when you **grow up?**

Kate: Oh, yes. That's still **a little way off,** but I know we'll always be friends.

A little way off *a short distance in the future; within a short distance*

Graduation is only **a little way off** now.
Let's keep walking; the ocean is only **a little way off.**

Come home *to go to or arrive at your house or apartment*

Would you like to **come home** with me and have supper?

Count on *to rely on, to trust*

Yuko is a good student. You can **count on** her to be prepared for every class.

Each other *one another, used to express a relationship between two people*

Lynn loves Mike. Mike loves Lynn. They love **each other.**

Give back *to return something*

I have to **give back** your book. I'll **give** it **back** tomorrow.

Go for a walk *to stroll leisurely, to take a stroll*

What a lovely day! Let's **go for a walk.**

Go out *to go with a friend or friends to a restaurant, to the movies, for a ride, etc.*

I asked Arlene if she wanted **to go out** to dinner.

Grow up *to mature, to reach maturity*

Children are often too eager to **grow up.**

Make friends (with)   *to become friends (with)*

We want to **make friends with** our new neighbors.

Make up   *to invent, to fabricate with words*

My grandmother could **make up** wonderful bedtime stories. She used to **make** them **up** all the time.

Run after   *to pursue*

The police **ran after** the thief.

Take away   *to remove, to take from*

The tax collector **took away** all my money.
He **took** it **away** yesterday.

1. Match each idiom with the correct definitions.

Definitions	*Idioms*
_____ to go outdoors	a. to count on
_____ to return	b. to make up
_____ to become friends with	c. to take away
_____ to invent, to fabricate	d. to give back
with words	e. to grow up
_____ to pursue	f. to make friends
_____ to remove	g. to go out
_____ to trust	h. to run after
_____ to mature	

2. Select the correct idiom needed to complete each sentence.

a. When I _____ , I'll become a doctor.
(1) come home   (2) go for a walk   (3) grow up
(4) go out

b. Let's _____ in the park.
(1) come up   (2) go for a walk   (3) grow up
(4) give back

c. I should _____ more stories to tell the children.

    (1) count on   (2) go for a walk   (3) run after
    (4) make up

d. The thief _____ my bike.

    (1) took away   (2) went for a walk   (3) grew up
    (4) made up

3. **Read the sentence using each substitution.**

  a. I always **count on** your ad.
                 you.
                 her being on time.
                 Frank's help.
                 myself to do it.

  b. In the evening we **go for a walk** in the park.
                                around our neighborhood.
                                around town.
                                in the woods.

  c. The two boys like **each other.**
    Ed and Mary love _____ .
    We don't often visit _____ .
    The two boys stopped and looked at _____ .
    The Giants and the Red Sox don't play _____ .

4. **Use the idiom in parentheses in a sentence each person might say.**

  a. Carlos and Carol had walked and talked. The sun was hot. Carol said, "I'm too tired. I can't walk to the ice cream parlor." But Carlos said, "Sure you can. _____ _____ ." (a little way off)

  b. Little Tommy ran outside to play. It was time for supper. His mother called, " _____ ." (to come home)

  c. Patty likes jewelry. Her friend had a new necklace. Patty took her friend's necklace. Her friend was angry. She said, "_____ ." (to give back)

  d. Lee didn't feel like cooking dinner. She wanted to go to a restaurant. She called her friend Cynthia and said, "_____ ." (to go out)

Lesson 2: Love and Affection

Interview

Everett and Marion Hale really know about love. They have been married for forty years. Everett and Marion have five children and twelve grandchildren.

Int: Marion, when did you first meet Everett? When did you first **fall in love with** him?

Marion: Oh, I knew him a long time before I **fell in love.** I **was fond of** Everett, but I wasn't **going with** him. Oh, he was so funny **in those days!** I think he was scared of my parents.

Everett: I was always nervous **in front of** Marion's parents. In fact, her parents were the reason we **broke up** so many times. Her parents almost **drove me away.** Many times I thought it was **all over** between us.

Marion: Everett! That's not so! We used to see each other almost every day. We **broke up** so often because it was so much fun to **make up.**

Int: Yes, yes. The old expression, "to kiss and make up," I believe.

Marion: **By and by** I couldn't **keep from** loving him. And I still do. I'd **go back** and do it again, if I had to.

All over   *completely finished*

That car almost hit me! I thought it was **all over** for me!

Be fond of   *to like, to care for, to have affection for*

Linda is such a sweet person. I'm very **fond of** her.

Break up   *to dissolve a friendship or loving relationship; to divorce (said of a married couple)*

Did you hear the news? Richard and Anne **broke up** last night.

By and by   *after a period of time, after a while*

At first I liked her. **By and by** I began to love her.

Call on   *to visit*

Let's **call on** Lucy this evening. We haven't seen her in weeks.

Drive (someone) away   *to chase away, to repel*

The dogs **drove away** the intruder. They **drove** him **away** yesterday.

Fall in love (with)   *to love (someone) deeply, to begin to love*

It happened so fast! I met Helen at the office party and immediately **fell in love**. And she **fell in love with** me.

Go back   *to return, to take back*

You can't **go back** to the party right now. Helen doesn't want to see you.
I wish I could **go back** to my childhood.

Go with   *to date regularly (usually to the exclusion of all others)*

I **went with** Lorraine for three years. Now I am **going with** Sarah.

In front of   *before, in the presence of*

Don't do that **in front of** the children!

In those days   *in the past, in years gone by*

In those days, people read a lot more.

Keep from   *to refrain from, to stop doing something*

To **keep from** smoking, I eat candy all day.

Make up   *to become friends or lovers again*

I had a fight with my daughter this morning, but we **made up** already.

Make up a story for each picture using the idioms provided.

Is it all over?

drive away, go back, in front of

_____
_____
_____
_____
_____
_____
_____

In those days

call on, be fond of, keep from, fall in love

_____
_____
_____
_____
_____
_____
_____

Bob and Sally go with each other

break up, by and by, make up

_____
_____
_____
_____
_____
_____
_____
_____
_____
_____

Lesson 3: Strangers

Interview

James Willis is a stranger in our town. He came from New York City. His company transferred him to our city. James will install a new computer system in the local plant. He will live in our city about a year. The interview took place in a local restaurant.

Int: James, I'd like to ask you some questions about what you think of our city.

James: Sure. What's **on your mind?**

Int: I know you're **new in town** and I would like to know your impressions of us. Do you have any problems adjusting to life here?

James: No, there are no real problems. As you know, people here **go out of their way** to be friendly. It's a nice town.

Int: I'm glad to hear it. Since you **come from** New York City, I thought you might **feel funny** in a small town.

James: Not really. In New York I **was used to** living **by myself.**

Int: We don't want that here! We don't want you **to feel left out.**

James: Oh, I don't **feel left out. As a matter of fact,** people here never **leave me alone! I'm** not **used to** so much attention.

Int: We just want you to **feel at home.**

James: I'm not complaining. The people here are very nice. It's just that I've **shook hands** so many times, my hand is sore. Look, I can barely hold my fork!

As a matter of fact   *in fact, really*

As a matter of fact, I rarely go to the movies.

Be new in town   *to be a stranger*

I want you to help him find a hotel. He **is new in town.**

Be on one's mind   *to occupy one's thoughts or attention*

Stanley loves her very much. She is always on his mind.

Be used to   *to be accustomed to*

Daniel **is used to** living alone.

By oneself   *alone, without help*

The Thompsons built their house **by themselves.**

Come from   *to originate in, to be born and reared in*

I come from a small town, but my wife **comes from** New York City.

Feel at home   *to feel comfortable, to feel at ease*

Everyone here is so friendly. I **feel right at home.**

Feel funny   *to feel uncomfortable, to feel ill at ease*

She's a strange person. I **feel funny,** when she's in the room.

Feel left out　　*to feel rejected or excluded*

When John wasn't invited to your birthday party, he **felt left out.**

Go out of one's way　*to make a special effort*

You should **go out of your way** to make a stranger feel at home.

Leave someone alone　*not to interfere with or interrupt, to permit to be alone*

Your mother is busy. Please, **leave her alone.**

Shake (someone's) hand　*greet another person by clasping right hands*

We **shook hands** when we met. Then he **shook** my **hand** when he left.

Exercises

1. **Complete the following scenes. Use the idioms in parentheses in each sentence you construct.**

    a. James seems worried. He cannot work effectively today. Harry sees James looking out the window. Harry asks James, "_____?" (to be on one's mind)

    b. At the meeting everyone wore a suit. George came to the meeting wearing sports clothes. After the meeting, George said, "_____ ." (to feel funny)

    c. Collier is a loner. He likes to take long walks alone. I asked him if he felt left out of things. Collier said, "_____ _____ ." (as a matter of fact, by oneself)

    d. Lois is new in town. Everyone is curious about her. Who is she? What does she do? Finally, someone asks Lois about her background. Lois answers, "_____." (to come from)

    e. The children were playing with a small snake. Their mother saw them and said, "_____ ." (to leave something alone)

2. Use the following idioms to complete the rhyming sentences.

> to be used to   to feel left out
> by myself   to go out of one's way
> to feel at home

a. The kitten is sitting way up on the shelf. Don't cry! I can get you down _____ .

b. Poor Larry can't dance. He has the gout. With everyone dancing, he _____ .

c. Now Harry could not even walk a straight line. "Excuse me," he said, "I _____ drinking wine!"

d. We want you to stay.
   We don't want you to roam.
   We'll _____ .
   To make you _____ .

Lesson 4: Disappointment and Regret

Interview

The interviewer talked with a small group of high school students. He asked them to tell the worst thing that ever happened to them.

Int: And what's the worst thing that ever happened to you?

Samuel: The worst thing that ever happened to me was when I broke up with my girlfriend. It almost **broke my heart.** Luckily, we **got back together.**

Int: And you. What's the worst thing that ever happened?

Millie: Nothing really bad has happened to me. But last month I failed my driver's test. I didn't study. It's my own fault. I really **let myself down.** Everyone **looked down on** me. It was so embarrassing.

Chris: The worst thing is to **be around** selfish people. And I **can't stand** phonies. They can't do anything except criticize. They find **fault with** everything you do.

96

Be around   *to be in the vicinity, to be in the presence of*

It's funny. When I'm **around** Elaine, I get nervous. Elaine also gets nervous when I'm **around.**

Break (one's) heart   *to hurt one's feelings deeply*

When Lee and I broke up, it almost **broke my heart.**

Cannot stand   *to despise, to dislike, to be unable to tolerate*

Margaret and David **can't stand** selfish people.

Find fault with   *to criticize, to complain about*

Don't **find fault with** others; they may **find fault with** you!

Get back together   *to be rejoined, to make up*

I was afraid that Ellen and Jim would get a divorce. I'm so glad they **got back together.**

Let (someone) down   *to disappoint, to fail, to desert*

Don't **let me down!** Do your best!

Look down on   *to despise, to scorn, to consider inferior*

Don't **look down on** other people. They may **look down on** you.

The interview with the high school students focused on insincere people.

Millie: I hate phonies, too. A phony pretends to be your friend, then tries to **take advantage** of you.

Frank: I don't care for phonies, either. They try to **show off** all the time. They **act like** they're so big.

Michelle: Well, I don't know. I **feel sorry for** people like that. I think that early in life they **got off on the wrong foot.**

Act like   *to imitate, to behave*

Joan **acts like** a spoiled child when she doesn't get her way.

Feel sorry for   *to sympathize with*

I **feel sorry for** Sylvia because she has a hard life.

Get off on the wrong foot   *to start poorly, to make a blunder*

When I'm in a foreign country, I always worry that I'll **get off on the wrong foot.**

Show off   *to attempt to attract attention (by displaying one's abilities or possessions)*

Don't pay attention to him. He's just **showing off.**

Take advantage of   *to profit at the expense of another; to impose upon*

Jessica isn't very kind. She often **takes advantage of** people.

Exercise

Construct a short story for each picture. Use the idioms listed under each picture.

show off, act like, get off on the
wrong foot

_____

_____

_____

98

look down on, find fault with, cannot stand.

_____
_____
_____

break one's heart, feel sorry for, get back together

_____
_____
_____

be around, take advantage of, let someone down

_____
_____
_____

 **Doing**

Lesson 1: Achievement and Getting Things Done

Interview

An independent insurance agent discusses achievement and success with the interviewer. His name is Thomas Neal. He has his own insurance agency which employs six people.

Interviewer: How do you manage to get so much done? You started with nothing. Now you have a successful insurance agency.

Thomas: First, you must **buckle down** and **get with it.** You have to work and work hard.

Interviewer: We all work hard, but not all of us **go** as **far** as you have.

Thomas: That brings us to the second step. You have to select your goals and objectives and **stick to** them. I have achieved the goals I **set out to** achieve.

Interviewer: So the secret of success is to set goals and objectives.

Thomas: Definitely. **Get in the habit of** setting goals. Develop a plan of action and **stick to** it.

Interviewer: Well, I'm going to **put those rules into practice.** Maybe I can get ahead, too.

Thomas: If you're going to **make good,** you can't **cut corners.** That's the third rule.

Interviewer: Right. I understand.

Thomas: You should talk to Professor Diaz. He's had a big influence on our local college. He's well **on his way** to becoming a major figure in education. Mark my words, Geraldo Diaz will **leave his mark** on our college. He's a real **go-getter.**

Buckle down   *to concentrate upon, to work hard*

If you are going to be successful, you must **buckle down** and do your school work.

Cut corners   *to economize (usually at the expense of quality)*

George's company lost its reputation for excellence by **cutting corners** in production. When you **cut corners,** you run the risk of making poor quality products.

Get in the habit of   *to become accustomed to*

Lately I **got in the habit of** leaving work early.

Get with it   *to adjust to, to become more proficient or skillful*

If you are going to become a success in your job, you had better **get with it.**

Go far   *to be successful, to accomplish a great deal*

Antonio and Belinda have opened a pizza parlor. They work hard and their pizzas are great. I think they'll **go far.**

Go-getter   *an ambitious, energetic person*

Sally knows what she wants out of life and she works hard for it. Sally is a real **go-getter.**

Leave (one's) mark   *to influence, to leave an impression upon*

Jack has changed the entire management system in our insurance company. He has **left his mark** on the whole corporation.

Make good   *to become successful*

It takes intelligence, integrity, and a sense of politics **to make good** in business today.

On (one's) way   *moving forward in one's career*

Inez was just promoted to supervisor with only two years' experience. She's **on her way.**

Put something into practice   *to execute, to carry out*

In theory this computer software should do the job, but I need **to put it into practice** to be sure.

Set out to   *to begin with the intention of*

Each student **set out to** learn to speak English well.

Stick to   *to persevere in, to continue*

When Leroy starts something, he **sticks to** it until it is finished.

Exercise

Complete the following paragraphs by making up sentences with the idioms in parentheses.

a. "My grades in English are getting lower," said Phil. "_____." (buckle down)

b. Food costs are rising. Gas prices are high. Clothes cost more than ever before. The mother told her children, "_____ _____." (cut corners)

c. The father agreed with the mother. "Yes," he said, "we must economize and not waste so much." The mother replied, "_____." (get in the habit of)

d. Phil thought about his English class. He realized he was weak in vocabulary. "Well," Phil thought, "_____ _____." (get with it)

e. Kathy plans to study computer science. She works for a computer company part-time. Kathy said to her boss, "___ _____." (go far)

f. Kathy's boss was impressed with her ambition. He said to her, "_____." (go-getter)

g. Kathy's boss talked to the president of the company at lunch one day. He talked about Kathy's ability. "Yes, sir," he said. "_____." (leave her mark)

h. Phil has been studying his English very hard for several weeks. His teacher was very impressed. She said, "_____ _____." (make good)

i. "Kathy and Phil have both made good," said their friends. "Phil is now a fine English student, and _____ _____." (on her way)

j. The mother and father have worked out their plans to economize. "Now," said the father, "_____ ." (put these plans into practice)

k. Richard really wanted to study French, but now he is not studying very hard. "Well," said his father, "_____ _____ , but you're not studying now." (set out to)

l. "Yes, Dad," said Richard, "I know what I have to do. _____ _____." (stick to)

Lesson 2: Schoolwork

Interview

The interviewer meets with Professor Gerald L. Buckles. He is chairman of the education department. The interviewer talks to Professor Buckles about the students' school work.

Buckles: The students go to class about six hours a day. After their classes, they are expected to study an additional four hours.

Interviewer: After six hours of classes and four hours of outside assignments, your students must be ready to **call it a day!**

Buckles: Yes. They're usually **all in** by the time they finish studying at night.

Interviewer: What happens if students can't do the work?

Buckles: You **flunk out.** You don't get a second chance.

Interviewer: That's rough.

Buckles: Well, this is a tough school. We have to be strict. It's hard for a small liberal arts college to compete with the top universities. Our students, however, will give any school **a run for their money.**

Interviewer: The slower students must find themselves **in a bind.**

Buckles: Well, yes. If we **do have a blind spot,** it's the heavy work load we give our students. Many of them get **bogged down** with all the work they have.

Interviewer: You think you're **on the right track?**

Buckles: Don't **get me wrong.** I know we could be **barking up the wrong tree.** We aren't perfect here. However, we are convinced that without a decent education, you can't **get to first base** in terms of success.

A run for one's money   *a close race or contest*

The New York Yankees won the World Series, but the Los Angeles Dodgers gave them **a run for their money.**

All in   *exhausted*

After working all day in the hot sun, Jim and I were **all in.**

Bark up the wrong tree   *to be on the wrong track or trail*

The automobile makers thought that people still wanted the large cars, but they were **barking up the wrong tree.**

Be on the right track   *to be following the correct idea or solution*

When Jane presented the plan to her supervisor, he assured her that she was **on the right track.**

Call it a day   *to quit for the day*

Okay, Jim, we've finished all of the paperwork the boss asked for. Let's **call it a day.**

Flunk out *to fail a course; to have to leave school because of poor grades*

Donna's grades were so low that she **flunked out** of school.

Get bogged down *to slow down, to become so entangled that further progress is impossible*

So many different people were contributing ideas to the project that the work got **bogged down.**

Get someone wrong *to misunderstand or misinterpret someone*

I hate hamburgers. Don't **get me wrong.** I like American food in general. I just hate hamburgers.

Get to first base *to make a good beginning or early progress*

The salesman tried to get the manager to buy a new copying machine, but he couldn't **get to first base** with her.

Have a blind spot *to be unable or unwilling to see defects in a person, plan, idea, and so on.*

Joan can see right through Geraldo, Sam, and me, but she **has a blind spot** as far as Rusty is concerned.

In a bind *in trouble, unable to free oneself*

Roy has so many debts and money problems that he's **in a bind** right now.

Exercise

Study each picture. Select one idiom for each picture and make a statement that helps describe the picture.

in a bind, all in, call it a day

get someone wrong, have a
blind spot, get to first base

be on the right track, get to
first base, a run for one's
money

bark up the wrong tree, get
bogged down, flunk out

107

Lesson 3: Working Together

Interview

The interviewer discusses with Albert Koyama and Karen Green how people work together. They are salespeople in Anderson's Shoe Store. Al is in charge of men's shoes. Karen is responsible for women's and children's shoes.

Interviewer: I know both of you work in different departments, but I assume you have to work together. Is there much cooperation between the men's department and yours?

Karen: Oh, yes. I like **to team up with** Al. He **does his part** and more. Al is always glad to **lend a hand** when **I have my hands full.**

Al: Yes, we watch out for each other. Karen **pitches in** when I'm busy. She helps me with my paperwork, too. When we **put our heads together,** we can finish it in half the time.

Interviewer: I understand that you're hiring a new saleswoman to help out in women's shoes.

Karen: Yes, she **comes on board** next week.

Interviewer: It must be hard trying to train a new employee when you're so busy. They are always making mistakes.

Karen: No, wait. You shouldn't **put people down** just because they're new and inexperienced.

Al: That's right. You can't blame a new employee for not **knowing the ropes.** And you can't **pass the buck** to someone new either. But the most important thing to remember, however, is that we're all **in the same boat.**

Karen: Right. You can't **count someone out without a fair showing.**

Interviewer: You're right. Cooperation and teamwork are important.

Al: Absolutely. Working together **makes a difference.**

Come on board — *to join or start work with a new team, company, organization, and so on*

We just hired Ellen Booth as our new financial officer. She'll **come on board** sometime next week.

Count someone out — *to consider someone incapable of participation*

Wait! I want to go with you. Don't **count me out.**

Do one's part — *to accept one's share of the work or responsibility*

You can't rely on Roger and Bill. They always **do their part.**

Have one's hands full — *to be very busy or occupied*

When you are rearing three children, you really **have your hands full.**

In the same boat — *sharing the same experience or destiny*

In our company sales people and production people work closely together. They realize that they are **in the same boat.**

Know the ropes   *to be experienced, to know the routine of*

Our school just hired a new English teacher. She's been teaching for over ten years and she **knows the ropes.**

Lend a hand   *to help, to assist*

I'm not sure how to fill out these sales forms, Marion. Will you **lend a hand?**

Make a difference   *to be of importance*

Studying English grammar is important, but practice in speaking really **makes a difference.**

Pass the buck   *to avoid responsibility for an action or decision by giving it to someone else.*

Although Harry was responsible for the mistake, he tried **to pass the buck** to Cindy.

Pitch in   *to help, to lend a hand*

In times of trouble in our town, everyone **pitches in** and we all work together.

Put our heads together   *to confer with each other*

No one could find the answer to the problem until we **put our heads together.**

Put someone down   *to humiliate someone, to make someone feel inferior or ashamed*

Nancy did the best she could. There is no reason for you to **put her down.**

Team up with   *to join up with someone for a special purpose*

Look, Tom. We're both working on the same problem. Let's **team up with** each other and solve the problem faster.

Without a fair showing   *not allowing a fair chance or opportunity*

Larry judged Ellen's work too quickly and dismissed her **without a fair showing.**

Exercise

Select the correct idiom for each sentence.

a. Let's cooperate. We're all _____ , you know.

   (1) passing the buck   (2) in the same boat
   (3) without a fair showing

b. Remember that in every situation, each person must _____

   _____ .

   (1) do his or her part   (2) come on board   (3) pass the buck

c. George said that it was Carol's fault. I think he _____

   _____ .

   (1) was without a fair showing   (2) was teaming up with her
   (3) passing the buck

d. Carol can take care of herself. She knows what George is
   doing. Don't _____ .

   (1) do her part   (2) count her out   (3) know the roles

e. That company offered me a job. They want me to _____
   _____ in a month.

   (1) come on board   (2) have my hands full
   (3) pass the buck

f. Consideration and kindness help us do business. These two
   things really _____ .

   (1) put heads together   (2) lend a hand
   (3) make a difference

g. Bob and Harry wanted to start a restaurant, so they _____
   _____ Jane.

   (1) have their hands full with   (2) teamed up with
   (3) put her down with

h. If you want to help, just _____ . There's plenty
   of work.

   (1) pitch in   (2) without a fair showing   (3) know the ropes

i. _____ his work cannot be judged. Give him a
   chance!

   (1) Put him down   (2) Lend a hand   (3) Without a fair
   showing

j. Don't _____ . She's doing the best she can.

   (1) lend a hand   (2) pitch in   (3) put her down

k. We can solve this problem. All we have to do is_____ .

   (1) be in the same boat   (2) count him out
   (3) put our heads together

l. We need an experienced person in this job, someone who___
   _____ .

   (1) is in the same boat   (2) knows the ropes
   (3) will lend a hand

m. Can you _____ ? I'm really busy right now.

   (1) put me down   (2) know the ropes   (3) lend a hand

n. Can you help me? I really _____ .

   (1) have my hands full   (2) pitch in   (3) do my part

Lesson 4: Supervising Others

Sherry Harley is the supervisor of nursing in a nursing home for the elderly. Her job consists of hiring new employees, evaluating job performance, and insuring that nursing operations run smoothly.

Interviewer: Thank you for seeing me, Ms. Harley. As you know, I'm studying how supervisors get others to work effectively through supervision.

Sherry: Yes, I see. Well, to me, supervision is mainly two things, leadership and **clear-cut** communications.

Interviewer: I see. Do you have any problems with your staff?

Sherry: As a supervisor I have a number of problems. Let's **run through** communications, for example. Good communication sounds easy, but it's hard.

Interviewer: Really?

Sherry: Oh, yes. **For my part,** I must be careful about the tone

as well as the clarity of my instructions. You can't **ride roughshod over** people, especially other nurses.

Interviewer: So tone is the most important thing.

Sherry: Again I must say it's tone and clarity. If your orders aren't **clear-cut**, everyone will be **running around in circles**. How can people do their jobs, if their instructions are vague? You **wind up** having to **do it all over** again.

Interviewer: So you communicate with your staff a lot.

Sherry: Absolutely. For example, we started a new procedure for diet control last month. I **filled in** each member of the staff **in depth**. That way, I only have to **keep an eye on** staff members occasionally, to be sure they **are carrying out** the new procedure correctly.

Interviewer: As a leader and supervisor you **take great pains** to communicate well.

Sherry: Yes. Careful communication can **work wonders!**

Carry out   *to perform assigned duties or tasks*

Whenever the captain gives an order, his soldiers immediately **carry it out**. They always **carry out** his orders perfectly.

Clear-cut   *clear and definite*

I don't understand why Henry was confused about what to do. The instructions were **clear-cut**.

Do something over   *to repeat a task*

That's not the way to write a financial report. **Do it over** until you get it right.

Fill someone in   *to provide someone with essential background information*

I missed the meeting yesterday afternoon. Could you **fill me in** on what happened.

For my part   *as far as I am concerned*

For my part, I won't support your sales plan at the next sales meeting.

In depth   *thoroughly and completely*

Mary Ann went over each function of the computer program **in depth.**

Keep an eye on   *to watch*

I have to go to the store for some milk. Could you **keep an eye on** the children while I'm gone?

Ride roughshod over   *to disregard the feelings of those around you*

Kate **rode roughshod over** everyone at the meeting. As a result no one was in favor of her plan for the annual dinner.

Run around in circles   *to be confused, to waste time in useless motion*

John forgot his shopping list. As a result he found himself **running around in circles** at the supermarket.

Run through   *to go through, to rehearse, to review*

Sherry had each nurse **run through** the steps in emergency treatment for heart attack.

Take (great) pains   *to proceed with great care and attention*

Joan **took great pains** to see that everyone was comfortable and relaxed at dinner.

Wind up   *to end up*

The lecture **wound up** fifteen minutes early, so we **wound up** taking a short test.

Work wonders   *to have miraculous results*

Have you tried that new vitamin combination? It **works wonders!**

115

Exercise

Study each picture. Select one idiom for each picture and make a statement that helps describe the picture.

keep an eye on, ride roughshod over, run around in circles

carry out, clear-cut, do something over

_____

_____

take (great) pains, run through, work wonders

for my part, fill someone in, in depth

_____

_____

Index

117

come to (one's) senses, 28
come up to, 57
come up (with), 65
count on, 85
count (someone) out, 109
crack a book, 41
crack up, 77
cross (one's) mind, 19
cry out for, 54
cry over spilled milk, 77
cut corners, 101
cut down on, 57
cut out for, 10

die of, 65
do (one's) best, 46
draw the line (at), 24
dream up, 24
drive (one) to drink, 77
drive (someone) away, 89
drop (someone) a line, 37

each other, 85
eat (one's) words, 14

far away, 46
fall in love (with), 89
feel sorry for, 98
feel at home, 93
fill in, 42
fill out, 42
find fault with, 33, 97
feel funny, 93
feel left out, 94
find out, 49
first of all, 46
flunk out, 106
fly off the handle, 74
for example, 57
for laughs, 69

from time to time, 49

get a kick out of, 69
get a word in edgewise, 14
get back, 46
get back together, 97
get bogged down, 106
get in the habit of, 101
get into, 65
get in touch with, 37
get mixed up, 19
get off on the wrong foot, 98
get sick, 62
get (someone/something)
    wrong, 6, 106
get the idea for, 58
get the picture, 28
get to first base, 106
get under (one's) skin, 69
get well, 62
get with it, 101
get worse, 62
give it to (someone) straight, 33
give (one) a free hand, 33
give (one's) word, 14
give (one) the benefit
    of the doubt, 33
give (someone) a hand, 53
give up, 50
go back, 89
go by, 65
go far, 101
go for a walk, 85
go-getter, 101
go into, 50
go nuts, 77
go off half-cocked, 74
go out, 85
go out of (one's) way, 10, 94
go steady, 69

118

take part in, 54
take pride in, 11
take (someone/something)
  with a grain of salt, 7
take steps, 29
thanks a lot, 47
think highly of, 7
think twice about, 24
think up, 58
to death, 77
to (one's) heart content, 70
to (one's) surprise, 50
turn around, 47
turn out, 79
turn back, 66
turn into, 66
turn off, 50
turn on, 50
turn out, 79

under (one's) breath, 15
under (one's) thumb, 7
up-to-date, 11

wade into, 82
want out, 70
wash off, 61
waste (one's) breath, 7
windbag, 3
without question, 29
work on, 50
work out, 58

yes-man, 3